University of Oxford

CW01663218

Japanese netsuke in Oxford

from the Ashmolean Museum
Pitt Rivers Museum
and the Museum of the
History of Science

O. R. Impey

Ashmolean Museum Oxford
1993

Text and illustrations © Ashmolean Museum, Oxford 1987
All rights reserved
ISBN 0 907849 72 5

Ashmolean Museum publications
Oriental art

Chinese Ceramics
Eastern Ceramics from the Collection of Gerald Reitlinger
Oriental Lacquer

British Library Cataloguing in Publication Data
Impey, Oliver
Japanese netsuke in Oxford
1. Netsukes
I. Title II. Ashmolean Museum
736'.68 NK6050

ISBN 0-907849-72-5

Cover illustration: A wooden figure of an actor, no. 31

Designed by Cole design unit, Reading
Set in Frutiger by Meridian Phototypesetting Limited
and printed in Great Britain by Henry Ling Limited,
The Dorset Press, 1987. Reprinted 1993.

Preface

This catalogue comprises a selection of the netsuke held in the collections of three Museums of the University of Oxford. The Ashmolean has a specialist collection of Japanese art, including the miniaturist works of art such as *inro* and netsuke. Many of the netsuke were given to the Museum by the late Sir Herbert Ingram in 1956; other gifts such as the Christie-Miller gift have followed, while yet others, promised, are not here included. The Pitt Rivers Museum holds the main part of the Hermann Gunther collection, presented by A.E. Gunther in 1974, while a special group of this collection, each member of which exhibits something of medical interest, comes from the same gift to the Museum of the History of Science.

The author of this modest booklet acknowledges with gratitude the cooperation of the Directors of the Ashmolean Museum, Sir David Piper and Dr. Christopher White and the Keeper of the Department of Eastern Art, Dr. James Harle, the Curators of the Pitt Rivers Museum, Dr. B.A.L. Cranstone and Dr. Schuyler Jones, and of the Museum of the History of Science, Mr. Francis Maddison. In these Museums, Miss Jane Christie-Miller, Miss Linda Cheetham and Dr. G.L'E. Turner have given material assistance. The photographs were taken by Mrs Geraldine Beasley of the Ashmolean's photographic service. Throughout the work on this booklet, the help of Mr. Neil Davey of Sotheby's, an acknowledged expert on netsuke and author of a standard text, has been invaluable.

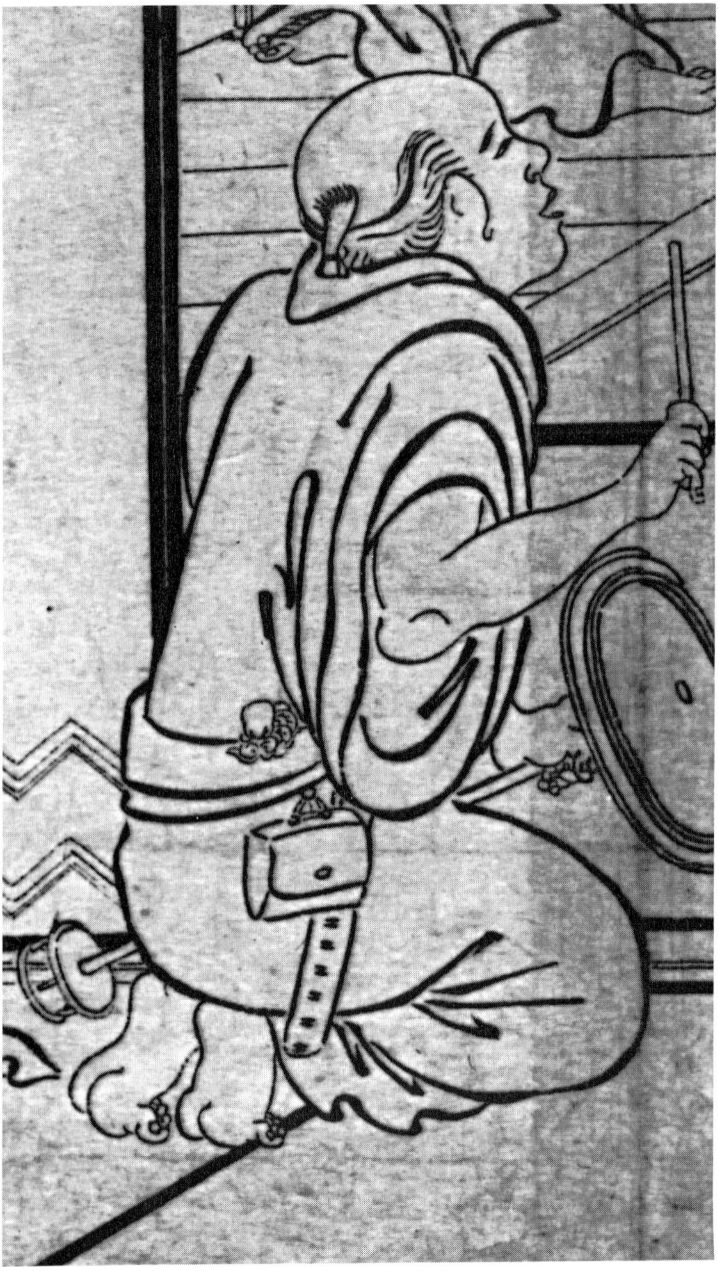

A netsuke in the form of an octopus in use, holding a tobacco pouch and pipe (see 65). Detail of a preparatory drawing for a woodblock print, triptych, by Torii Kiyonaga (1752–1815). The Rijksmuseum, Amsterdam.
Drawing 56.226A
Gift of F. Lieftinck

One of the most keenly collected of all Japanese works of art are the charming small sculptures called netsuke. These are, and were, not sculptures to be placed on a surface and looked at, they were for use, for a specific purpose, and this, of course, has not only governed their small size, but also has placed certain other constraints upon the carver.

The need for these carvings is simple. Japanese dress has, or had, no pockets. In order to carry minor items about their persons, Japanese men and women had only three possibilities, either they could place a flat object in the crossed fold of the kimono, they could carry small items in the sleeve, or they could use the belt or sash, the *obi*. The Samurai stuck his two swords, curved cutting edge upwards, through this *obi*; the townsman, the *chonin*, suspended small items below the *obi* by means of a cord. This cord was tucked up into the *obi* and held in place by the netsuke which was, therefore, in effect a sort of toggle-button.

That netsuke became minor works of art is due to the circumstances of the users of netsuke in the Edo, or Tokugawa period (1603–1868) during which time most netsuke of any quality were made. Shifting patterns of power in Japan in the sixteenth century had caused profound economic changes. Whereas the landed aristocratic families had dominated an economy based on rice, in the seventeenth century the growth of towns threw up a new merchant class using an economy of money. From the seventeenth century until the middle of the nineteenth century, the de facto government of Japan, controlled by the Tokugawa family ruling in the name of the Emperor, pursued a policy of self-imposed isolation from the rest of the world. All trade and contacts with foreign countries were prohibited, save through the rigidly controlled ports of, at first, Hirado and then Nagasaki on Kyushu island, the southernmost of the Japanese islands.

Under these circumstances, the country was peaceful after centuries of intermittent civil war. The *samurai* class were virtually unemployed, and were debarred from almost all forms of activity that could be remotely commercial. Thus they rapidly got into debt to the merchants, who became increasingly rich but never powerful. Edicts governing the movement of the families of the great aristocracy ensured that they spent at least half of their time in Edo (modern Tokyo) and their families remained there almost as hostages: this system, analogous to that used by Louis XIV in

France, ensured maximum expenditure on luxurious living. This in turn ensured a plentiful supply of craftsmen who could create the luxuries demanded.

But these craftsmen, and the merchants who controlled their commercial activities were themselves debarred by continual sumptuary edicts from indulging in luxuries. Even their dress was regulated though it must be admitted that such edicts were often flouted.

Whereas the upper classes could use silk for their dress and gold on their sword furniture, the merchant classes were forced to use more humble materials. But rich merchants and their like had to have some form of conspicuous consumption: they managed this by the creation of fashions for elaborately made minor masterpieces of non-luxurious materials, where the luxury was the skill and time of a fine craftsman usually working in wood, or lacquer: ivory seems also to have been permitted.

The two items that best met those requirements were the netsuke and the items which it served to hold in place. There were three items most commonly suspended from the *obi*; the *inro* (literally, box for seals) which was a small wooden box of interfitting tiers, usually lacquered, the pipe-case and tobacco bag, and the brush and ink holder. Much the most widely used of these was the *inro*, which usually held the various herbal medicines that the Japanese considered so vital; this itself became one of the most elaborate and beautiful of the Japanese minor arts, allowing the full range of exceedingly sophisticated lacquering techniques to be exploited on a miniaturist scale. Doubtless, inro were the subject of contemporary connoisseurship and competitive collecting, just as jewelled snuff-boxes (themselves sometimes inlaid with Japanese lacquer) were in Europe in the 18th-century. So also were netsuke.

Netsuke are made to hang above the *obi*. They must not be so large, or of such an awkward shape as to catch in the clothing, nor must they be too heavy. In general, netsuke tend to be compact, rounded sculptures, though there are elongated forms, where the very length was exploited not only as part of the sculptural form but also to hang low down over the *obi*, thus being conspicuous and remaining upright – such pieces are nearly always models of standing figures. Naturally such netsuke are somewhat bigger than the norm, being often 12 or 15 cm. long. The more rounded forms of netsuke tend to be about 4 cm. wide.

The placing of the holes for the cord to run through is a vital part of the design of a netsuke. Usually a passage is cut through the model with one entrance hole larger than the other to conceal the knot of the cord from which suspends the inro or other fitting. Sometimes the model is so carved that if it is an animal, say, then the hole will be that space between a leg and the body, or in the loop of the tail. It is absolutely vital that the cord holes are so placed that the netsuke looks well when hung at the *obi*, that it stays the way up that was intended.

There are five main types of netsuke. By far the most common is the sculptural rounded form, *katabori*; very often this is an animal, equally often a figure of some historical, legendary or symbolic subject. The second shape we have already considered, the elongated *sashi* netsuke which usually depicts a foreigner of exaggerated form. Thirdly there is the rounded *manju* ('bean cake') netsuke, which is often more perfunctorily carved than the normal and fourthly the *kagamibuta*, where there is a metal plate let into a wooden or ivory disc, through which the cord runs to attach to a loop fused onto the back of the metal plate. The metal plate bears the decoration. The fifth type of netsuke is simply a miniature theatrical mask. Each of these types of netsuke must perform the same function, in their different ways. Thus each will have a method of attaching the cord appropriate to the shape. This may be a hole cut through the netsuke, or a concealed loop – it is called the *himotoshi*.

Most *katabori* netsuke are of wood or ivory, though many other materials were used on occasion. The Japanese have a long tradition of wood-carving, mostly for Buddhistic subjects, as there is little stone suitable for monumental sculpture to be found in Japan. It may well have been the carvers of miniature shrine-figures for private household shrines who first carved netsuke. Many different woods are used, from imported ebony through native dark and close-grained woods and pale close-grained woods such as box to the softer woods such as cypress and cherry that could not be used for fine detail.

Ivory, imported into Japan by the Chinese, was expensive, and the tusks were cut up into triangular sections to avoid waste. In early *sashi* netsuke this triangular shape was not disguised (as it often was later) but was exploited by the carver to achieve the affect he wanted. Other 'ivories' than elephant-ivory were also used – walrus tusk, sperm-whale tooth and, later, hippopotamus tooth. These are often difficult to identify and can sometimes be found in catalogues described as 'marine ivory'.

Less commonly, other materials were used, boar tusk, stag's horn (a speciality of the Asakusa school), bone, Hirado porcelain (both these two only towards the end of the Edo period, or after Edo) lacquered wood, fossil wood, coral and natural *objets trouvés* such as dried crane's feet, or nuts. Sometimes, too, other minor works of art such as Chinese seals or small jades could be adapted and adopted as netsuke.

In addition, carved netsuke often have details of other materials

– eyes inlaid in coral or horn, details of dress in pearl-shell or stained bone. The Shibayama family, best known for their large showy ivory pieces, made some netsuke in which there are large inlays of different materials that form the decoration on a netsuke, and other makers sometimes used such large inlays, too.

Manju netsuke are usually of ivory, though wood or lacquered wood occurs. Manju themselves are of three main types, all of flattened rounded outline. One type is a ring of ivory through the centre of which is a small plug, which at the back forms the *himotoshi*. The second type is carved and pierced in low relief in the round. And the third type is in two halves, which fit together as hollow discs, the cord running through the plate which is the back to reach the *himotoshi* which is attached to the back of the front disc; in this respect it resembled the *kagamibuta*.

Kagamibuta have a metal plate, with the *himotoshi* at the back, held in the mouth of an ivory (or occasionally wood) cup which has a hole at the back through which runs the cord. The face of the plate is decorated in the techniques used for sword-furniture; flat inlay (*hirazogan*) raised inlay (*takazogan*) or incising to imitate brush-strokes (*katakiri*) into a soft metal background such as *shakudo* or *shibuichi*. Sometimes such pieces even imitate *tsuba*. In the Meiji period, when the wearing of swords was banned, many makers of sword-furniture were rendered redundant, and had to turn to the making of other things; one of these was the *kagamibuta* plate.

Mask netsuke, imitating theatrical masks, are seldom so accurate that one can presume a connection between theatrical mask carvers and netsuke makers – rather they seem pastiches of real masks. The *himotoshi* is formed by a bar across the hollow back of the mask.

Netsuke were probably first used in the 16th or 17th century, though evidence of them is lacking even in contemporary paintings that show townspeople; it must be presumed that when first used they were, simply, toggle buttons. The word netsuke, meaning 'root attachment' suggests this simplicity. So the earliest netsuke known are of the eighteenth century, and the very numbers of these that exist suggest a boom in the fashion for these carvings, especially in the large and growing town centres of Edo, Osaka and Sakai, while thriving schools of netsuke carvers were to arise in Kyoto, Nagoya and various provincial centres such as Hida and Iwami.

In general the early netsuke are large and boldly carved, often of inventive form and frequently of satirical or humorous content. As in other Japanese art-forms, an irreverent, teasing humour with a strong element of caricature is often present. Later there is a tendency towards miniaturisation and towards virtuoso carving, which reaches high peaks in the works of such artists as Kaigyokusai, or Ichimin. At the end of the Edo period, with the arrival of unrestricted western trade the general tendency of the Meiji period is followed in netsuke; on the one hand, superb quality works continued to be produced by great carvers for connoisseurs, and on the other hand thousands of carvings of the crudest quality and of inferior materials were mass-produced for the credulous west.

Today there has been a revival of interest not only in old netsuke, which have been keenly collected since the middle of the last century, but also in new work, and there are a number of artists in Japan producing excellent netsuke today, as well as a handful of westerners carving netsuke of a quality to compare with the best. Such a one is Michael Webb, whose work was exhibited in the Ashmolean in 1983, and who works in Yorkshire.

Crafts everywhere tended (until recently, perhaps) to run in families – a craftsman passed on his experience and techniques to his sons or sons-in-law; the latter were frequently favoured pupils. Nowhere was this more true than in Japan, where even painting ran in families (the Kano and Tosa families, for example). Netsuke carvers were no exception, and schools arose as masters acquired assistants and pupils. Just as in the other arts, the favoured pupil who was to become the next master would take the master's name or at least one character from his name (in practice, this was his *go*, or work-name). The most obvious and frequently quoted example of this (it occurs in the *Soken kisho* of Inaba Tsuryu, the first book to discuss netsuke, published in 1781) is the descent from *Tomotada* to his pupils *Tomo*tane and Oka*tomo*, the latter of whom has a brother *Oka*tori.

The schools, although distinct in their physical presence, in practice overlapped in materials, subjects and techniques, and it is usually impossible to assign an unsigned netsuke to a particular school and even more rarely to a particular artist. This throws into some doubt the validity of the school groupings and as unsigned netsuke are more commonly found than signed pieces this causes difficulties of classification.

Furthermore, signed pieces must be treated with caution. Artists would sometimes sign a pupil's work, or pupils use the master's signature, which adds to the difficulties, while even in their lifetime the finest artists were fraudulently copied by carvers with no connection to the school of the master. Buffaloes 'by' Tomotada, for instance, works of good quality, are far too common even to be school works. In general, signed works are attributed or not to the artist by connoisseurship, on grounds of quality, a method which may or may not be entirely valid, but which begs many questions.

The entries are approximately chronological. The *katabori* netsuke, the main body of the collections, come first, with only the Asakusa School especially grouped together, at the end of the 19th century preceding the two 20th century pieces. These are followed by the *manju*, by the *kagamibuta*, and by one *kagamibuta* with its pipe, pipe-case and tobacco pouch.

No measurements are included as all the illustrations are approximately actual size with the exception of no. 65.

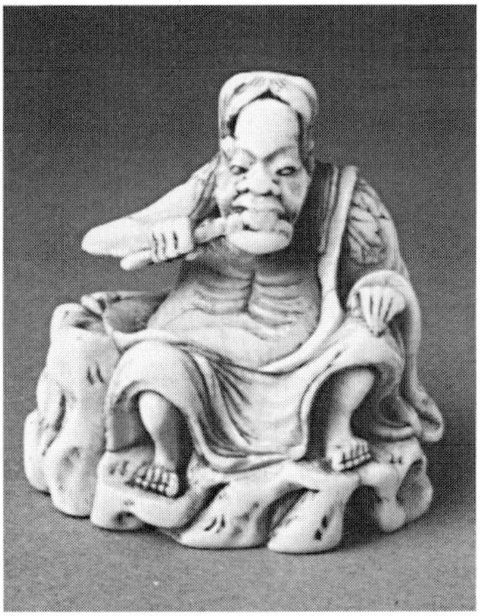

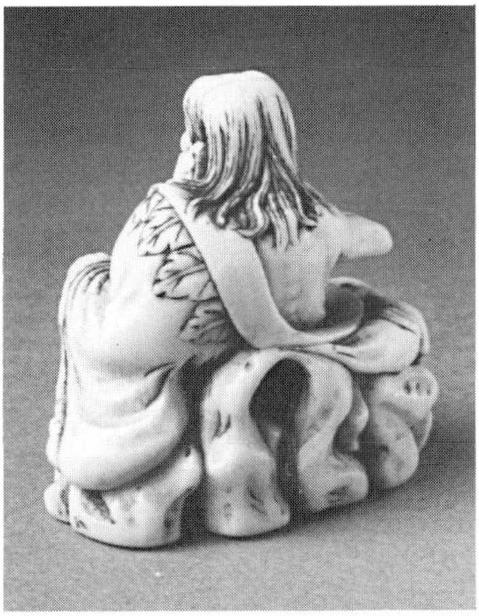

1 Ivory. The *sennin* Shinno seated on a rock holding with his right hand a medicinal herb on which he is chewing. Unsigned. Early 18th century.

• The Chinese emperor Shen Nung, credited as one of the inventors of the arts of writing botany and medicine, is honoured in Japan as Shinno.

Museum of the History of Science 2150

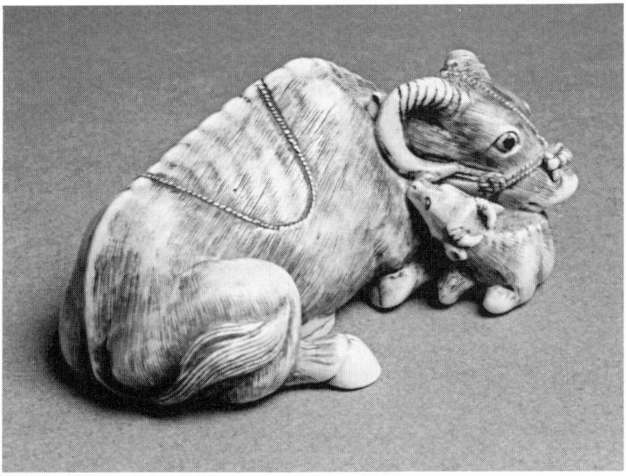

2 Ivory. A buffalo and her calf, she lies on her left side, her legs tucked underneath and with her chin resting on the calf. A rope halter is on her head, and reaches back over her hindquarters. The hair work incised in fine lines. The himotoshi has two large holes underneath.

Inscribed in an oblong cartouche *Tomotada*.

• Although clearly not by the master, this is a good 18th century essay in the style by a Kyoto-school carver.

Ashmolean 1963.160
Bouch bequest

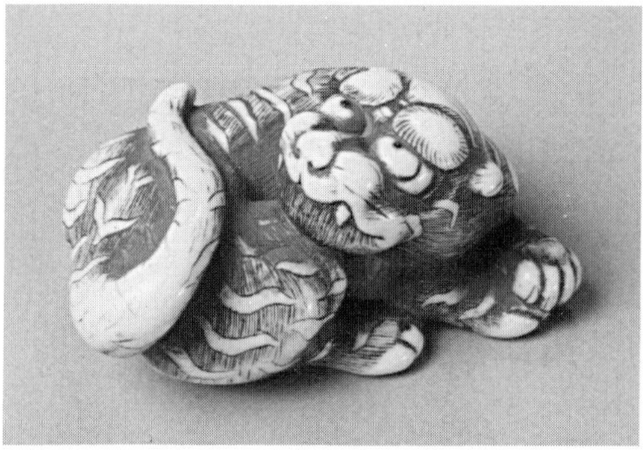

3 Ivory. A recumbent tiger looks up over its right shoulder, the hairwork engraved.
18th century.
• A good Kyoto school work of the 18th century.
Pitt Rivers 705

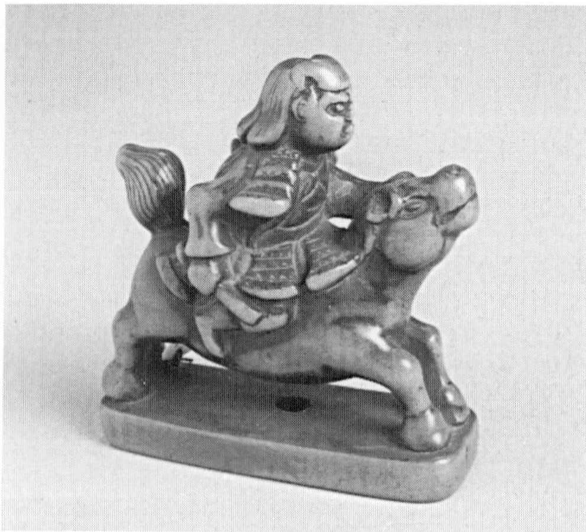

4 Wood. Soga no Goro riding his horse *ventre à terre*, on a rectangular base pierced to form the himotoshi.
Unsigned. 18th century.
• One of the Soga brothers riding in haste to meet his brother, Juro, before the revenge killing of the murderer of their father.
Pitt Rivers 221

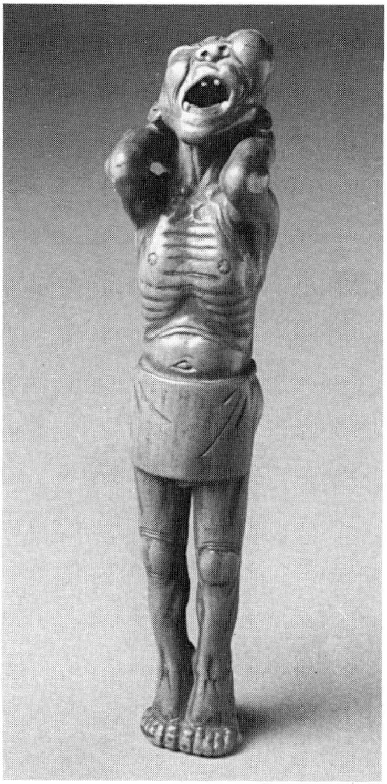

5 Wood. A *sashi* netsuke. A tall emaciated man standing on tiptoe and clutching the back of his neck in the agony caused by a huge swelling which closes his left eye, with ivory teeth. Signed *Yukoku*. 18th century.

• The apron that he wears suggests that he is not of Japanese origin, but may be from Micronesia.

Museum of the History of Science 2399

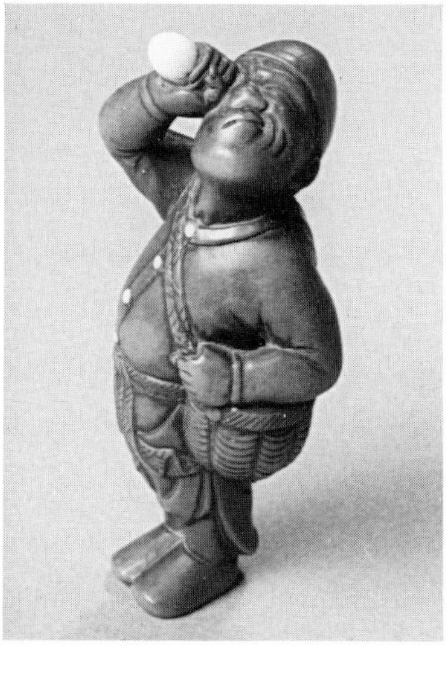

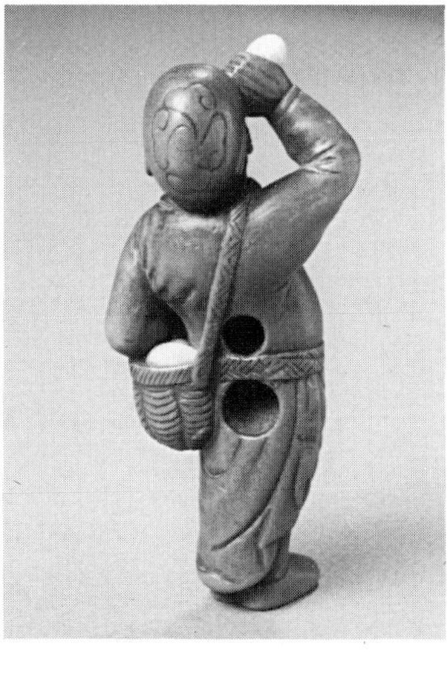

6 Wood and ivory. An egg-seller with a basket of eggs holds one to his right eye to verify its freshness by its translucency. Signed *Tanri*. 18th century.

Museum of the History of Science 2053

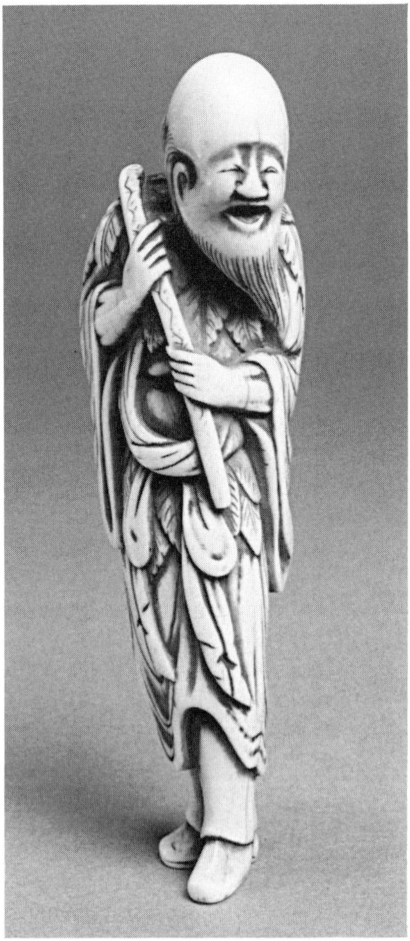

7 Ivory. A large upright figure of the *sennin* Tekkai as an old beggar with a staff and a cloak made of leaves, blowing his spirit into space through his open mouth. Unsigned. Late 18th century.

- This is an early netsuke, made of a triangular section of ivory, and so made that it is capable of standing upright on the sennin's feet.
- Tekkai is one of the eight Taoist immortals. Having been called to heaven to discourse with Laozu, his spirit was unable to enter his own body and was forced to enter that of an old beggar who had just died.

Ashmolean 1959.81
Christie-Miller gift

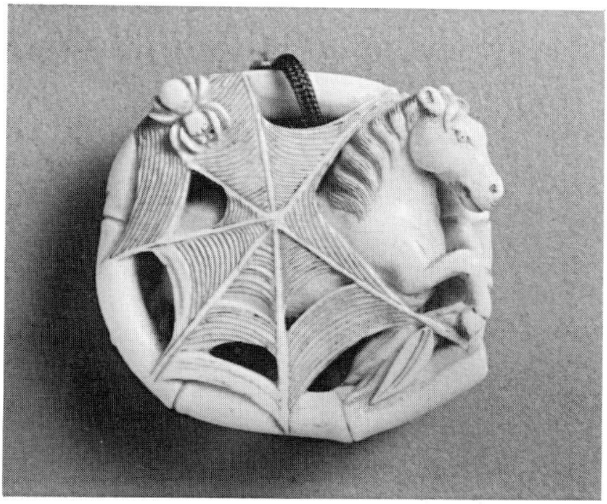

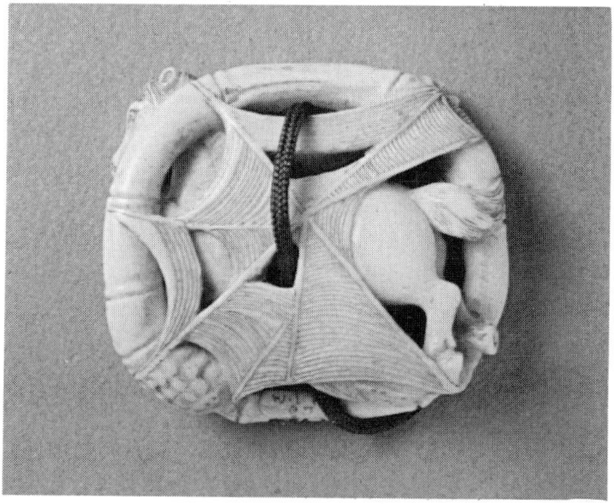

8 Ivory. A horse struggles to clear itself from a spider's web that is constructed within a curl of bamboo, the spider watching. Unsigned. Late 18th century.

• The subject illustrates the small events which alter the course of destiny.

Ashmolean 1956.1710
Ingram gift

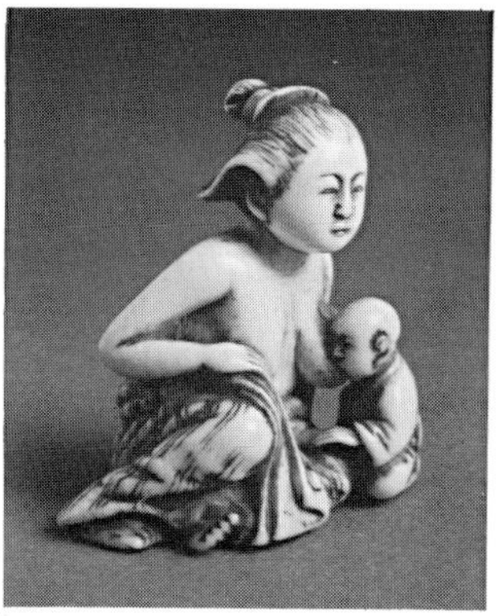

9 Ivory. A seated woman, naked to the waist suckles her son. Unsigned. Late 18th century.
Museum of the History of Science 447

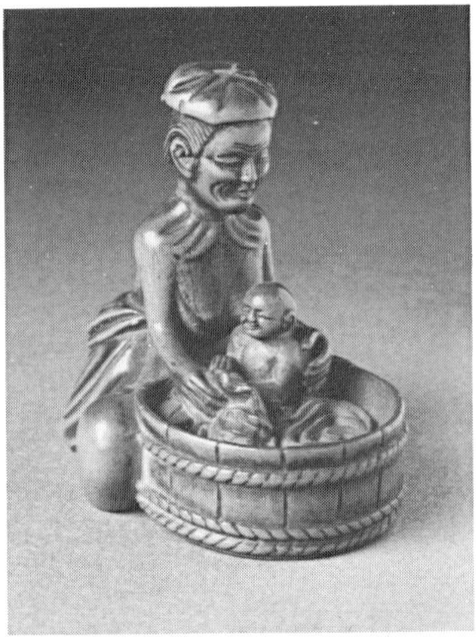

10 Wood. An old woman crouched before a water tub, bathes her grandson. Unsigned. Late 18th century.
Museum of the History of Science 2335

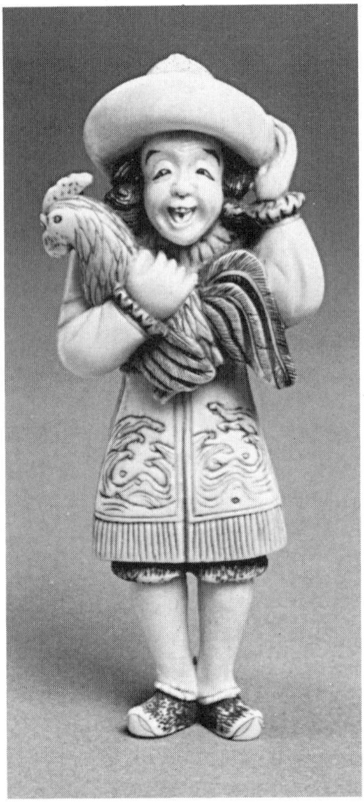

11 Ivory. A tall figure of a Dutchman wearing a frock coat and a wide-brimmed hat which he clutches in his left hand. In his right hand he holds a fighting-cock pressed closely to his chest, while he laughs aloud. Unsigned. Late 18th century.
- An early netsuke made from a long triangular section of ivory. The netsuke can stand upright on its feet.

Ashmolean 1956.3200
Ingram gift

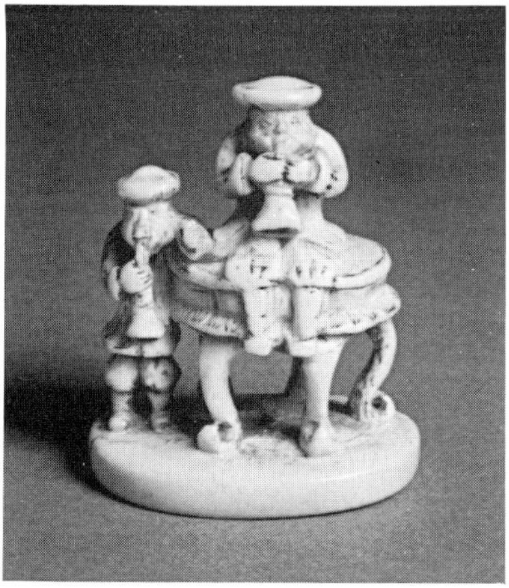

12 Ivory. Two Dutchmen playing wind instruments. One is seated on a table and uses both hands on the instrument, the other stands to the right, using only his right hand to play, while he beats time with his left.
The netsuke stands on a base, through which a hole forms the himotoshi.
Unsigned. Late 18th century.
Ashmolean 1956.3218
Ingram gift

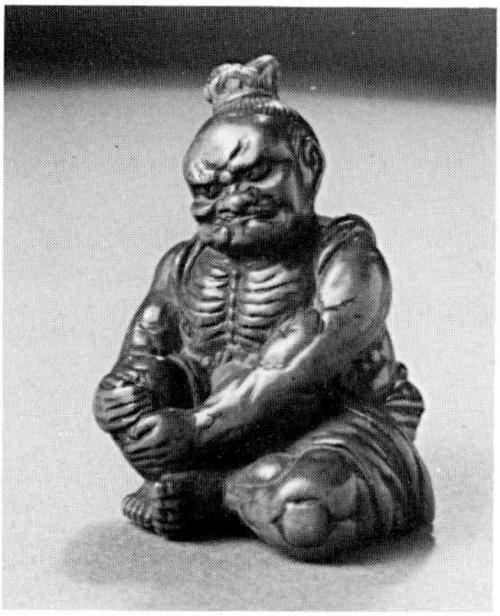

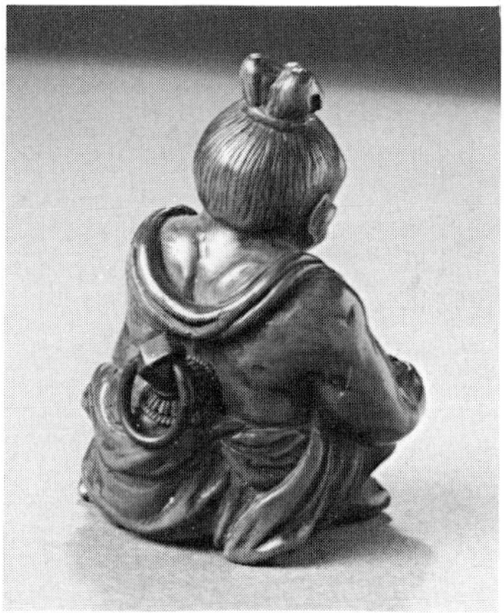

13 Wood. A grimacing *nio* holds his right knee in pain from the application of *moxa*. The himotoshi formed as a metal ring attached to his back.
Signed *Higo*.
Kameya Higo (active before 1781) lived in Osaka, carving netsuke as an amateur. He was a machinist and a dentist.
• Perhaps a suggestion that even the two Guardian Kings, who traditionally guard the doors of Temples, suffer from this painful remedy.
Museum of the History of Science 1904

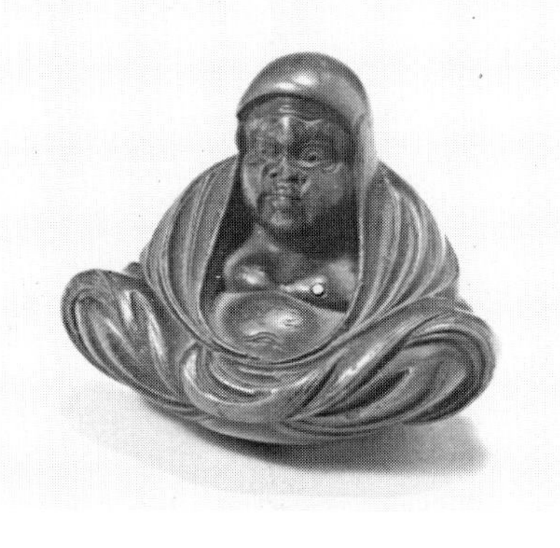

14 Wood. Daruma in characteristic meditating pose. The himotoshi well formed under the base.
Incised signature. *Shumin*.
Hara Shumin (active c.1789-1800) was a Tokyo artist who worked in wood and specialised in compact figural studies.
• For a humorous treatment of the legend of Daruma, see 15.
Ashmolean 1956.3202
Ingram gift

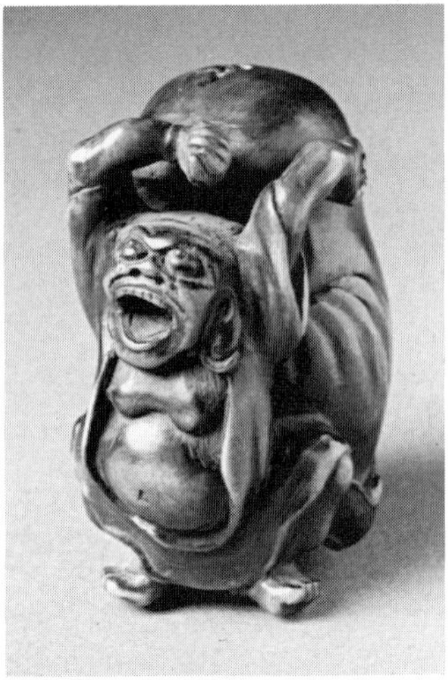

15 Wood. Daruma stretching his arms above his head and yawning hugely as he leaves his accustomed cloak and seated position of meditation.
Signed on a raised ovoid cartouche *Tadatoshi*.
Tadatoshi (1781–1800) worked in Nagoya.

- For Daruma in his normal pose of meditation which he held so long that he lost the use of his arms and legs, see 14.

Ashmolean 1956.1725
Ingram gift

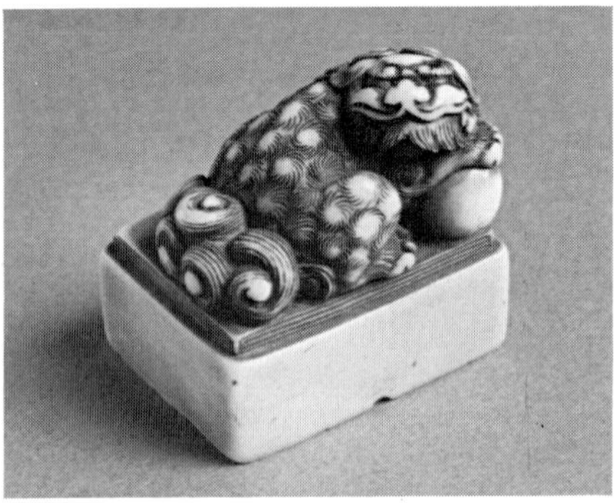

16 Ivory. A shishi, one forepaw on a ball, looks menacingly over its shoulder as it crouches on the square base of a seal.
Unsigned. 18th century.

- The seal could be read 'Brush, ink, song, dance' a celebration of four accomplishments.

Ashmolean Museum 1982.49
E.H. North bequest

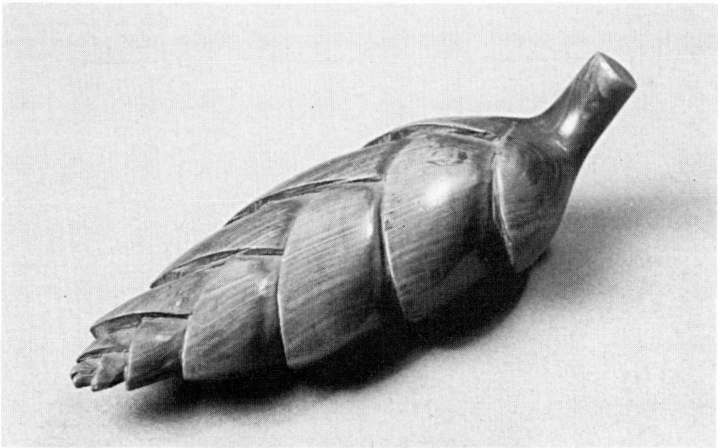

17 Wood. A shoot of ginger (*myoga*), used both for culinary purposes and as a medicinal plant said to induce absent mindedness.
Unsigned. Late 18th century.
Museum of the History of Science 1948

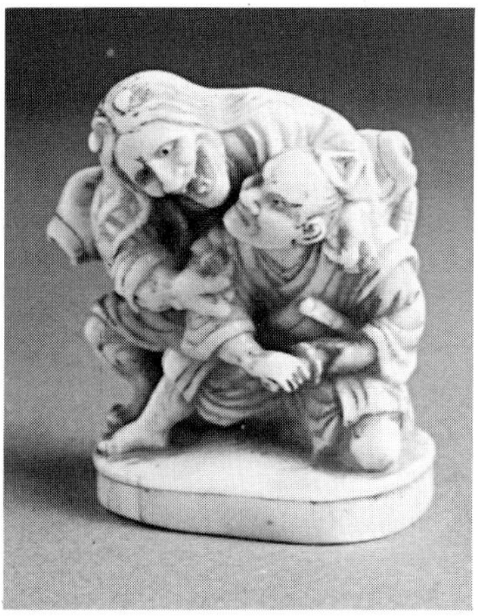

18 Narwhal ivory. Koremochi, on an ovoid base awakes from his drunken slumber and draws his sword to defend himself from a frightful witch who attacks him from behind with her clawed hands.
Unsigned. Early 19th century.
• The story is told in the Noh play Momijigari (maple picnic).
Ashmolean 1959.78
Christie-Miller gift

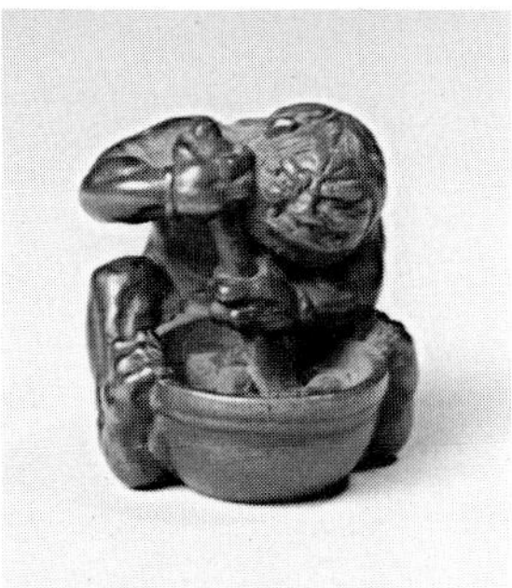

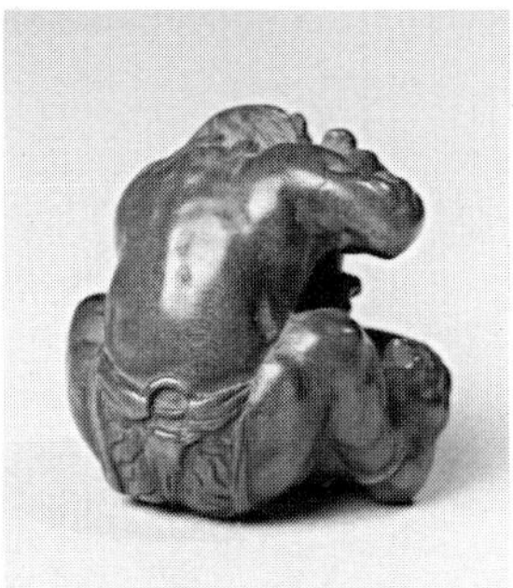

19 Wood. A seated demon clutching a mortar with his clawed toes pounds sinners with his pestle.
Signed *Kokei*.
Kokei was a pupil of Tanaka Minko, working in the town of Tsu during the first quarter of the 19th century.
• A representation of Hell taken from Chinese legends.
Ashmolean 1976.11
Christie-Miller gift

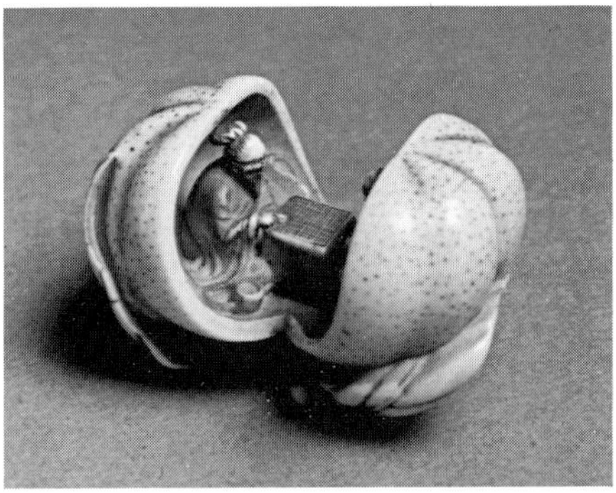

20 Ivory. A lobed fruit split in half to reveal two bearded men playing *go*. Unsigned. Early 19th century.
Ashmolean 1976.38
Christie-Miller gift

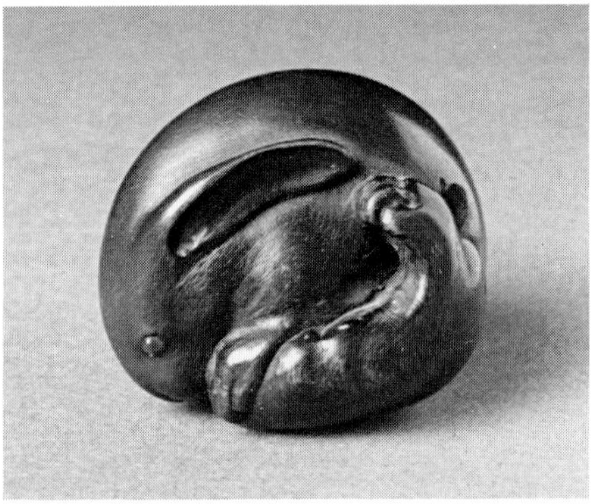

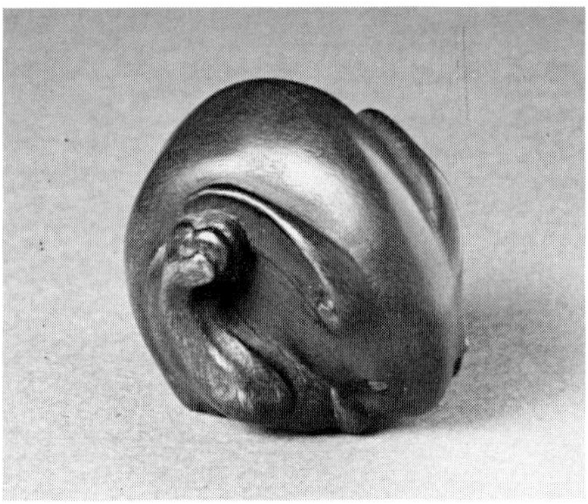

21 Wood. A rabbit, curled up to groom its hindquarters. The right hind leg is raised up to its right ear in the effort to reach the tail.
Incised signature *Ichimin*. Ichimin (active 1818–1839) worked in Nagoya.

- The himotoshi lies between the left hind leg and the body and shows signs of being later work. If this is so, then this netsuke originally had no himotoshi and was therefore useless.

Ashmolean 1956.3267
Ingram gift

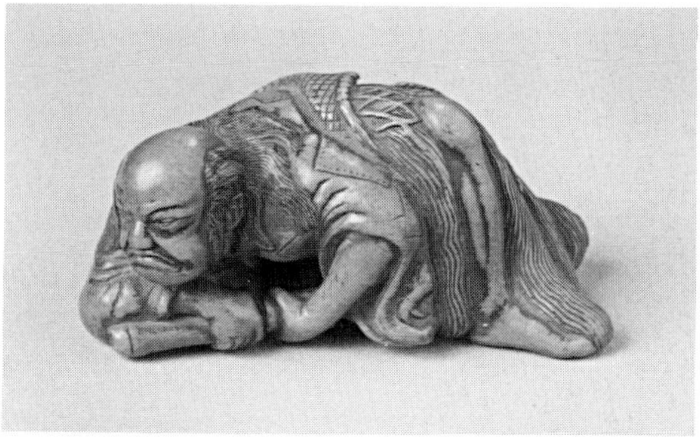

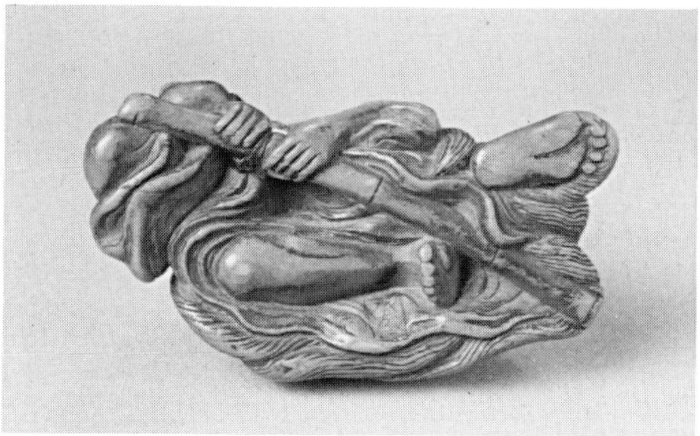

22 Wood. A *ronin* warrior crawling along the ground, his right hand ready to draw his sword.
Inscribed *Tomokazu*.
Not by Tomokazu, the artist of 35.
- After a model by Ogasawara Issai illustrated in Soken Kisho, where it is called a *Haiyu* (actor).

Pitt Rivers 578

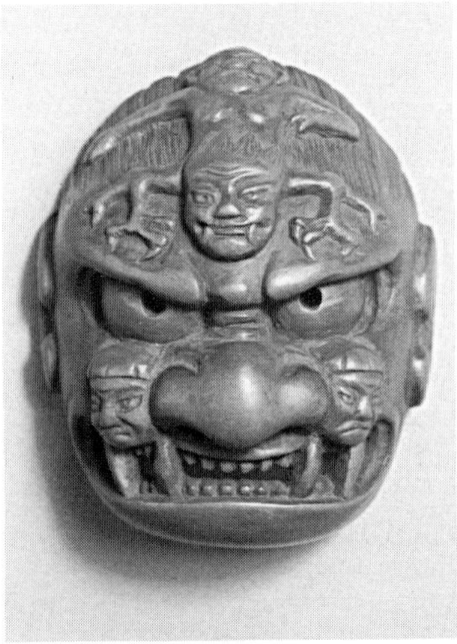

23 Wooden mask. A ferocious demon mask (Genkoji Kamen) with other demons who appear from between the canine teeth, and from the top of the head. Inscribed *Deme*.
The Deme family were well known theatrical mask makers.
Pitt Rivers 296

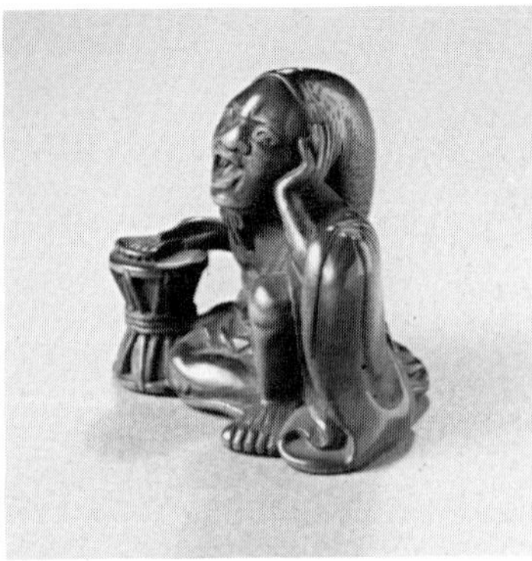

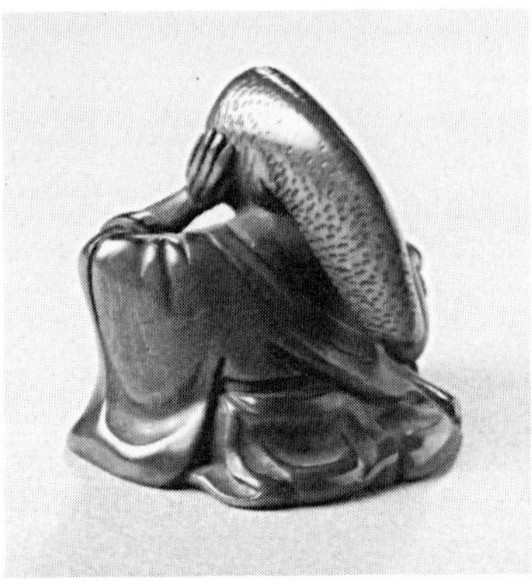

24 Wood. A musician wearing an enormous *eboshi* hat, kneeling beside his drum, holds his left hand to his cheek to alleviate the tooth-ache that contorts his features. Signed *Miwa* with *kakihan*.
There were several artists of his name, the earliest being mentioned in Soken Kisho in 1781. This excellent carving is likely to be early – mid 19th century.
Museum of the History of Science 1953

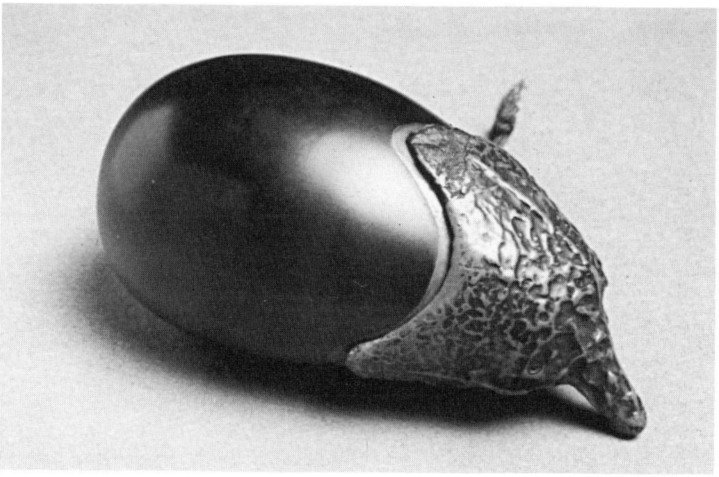

25 Lacquered wood. An aubergine of ovoid form with stalk and bracts of rough red lacquer, most realistically worked. The stalk attachment is removable and the himotoshi attachment comes out of the body, the cord running through the vegetable.
Signed in red lacquer on the inner attachment *Joshin*.
An apparently unrecorded artist.
Ashmolean 1956.3026
Ingram gift

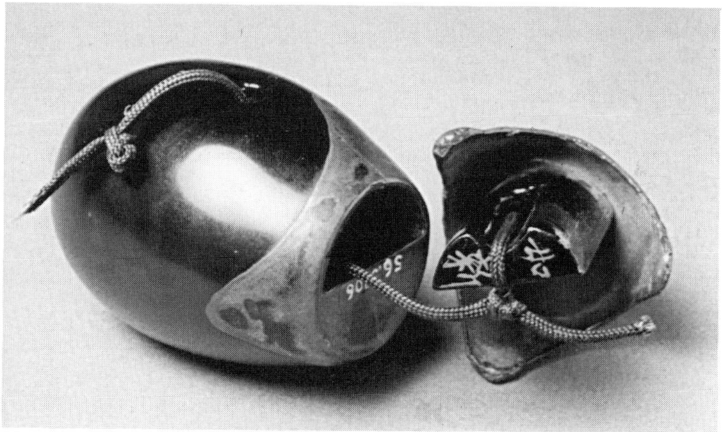

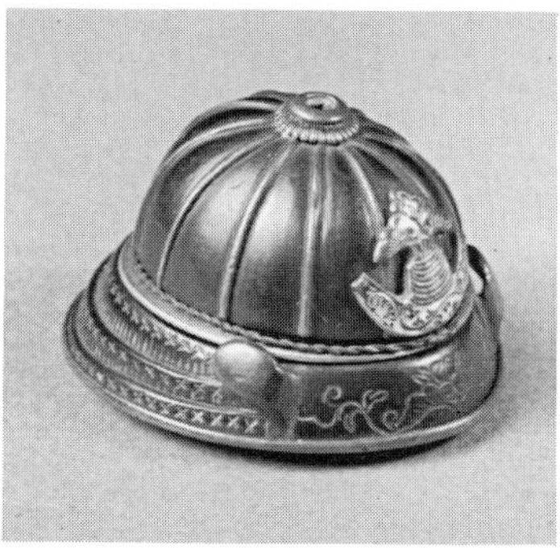

26 Metal. A helmet in *shakudo*, of twelve plates with gilded *mon* and gilded and incised detail. The three-layered *shikoro* removable to reveal the attachment for the himotoshi.
Unsigned. 19th century.
The helmet has a 12 plate *sujibachi* style bowl.
Ashmolean 1956.3224
Ingram gift

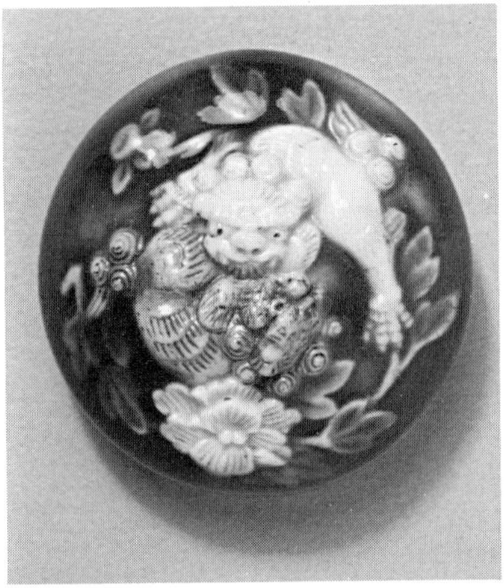

27 Porcelain manju. Two relief-modelled shishi in white and iron-brown fighting, on an underglaze blue ground. Hirado porcelain.

- The Hirado porcelain kilns at Mikawachi on Kyushu seem to have begun about 1770. By the end of the century Hirado produced the best quality porcelain made in Japan at that time. Production continued throughout the 19th century, reaching a peak of sophistication in the 1830s–50s.

Pitt Rivers 817

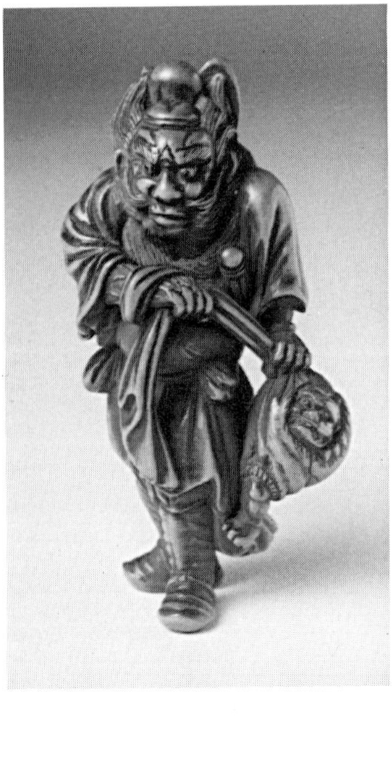

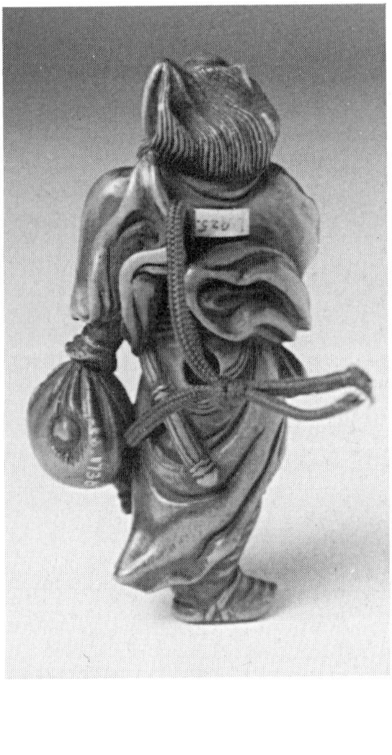

28 Wood. Shoki, the demon queller, stands upright drawing tight a bag from which a demon struggles to escape. Signed, in an irregular cartouche *Taguchi*.
A fine example by this artist whose work appears to be very rare.
Ashmolean 1956.1730
Ingram gift

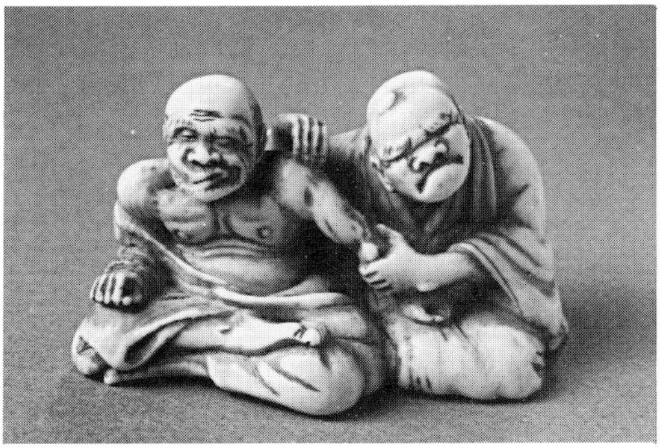

29 Ivory. A blind masseur (with a cyst on his head) wrenches the left arm of his patient, clearly causing some pain.
Signed *Yoshikazu*.
Yoshikazu was an Edo school artist of the mid 19th century.
Museum of the History of Science 2346

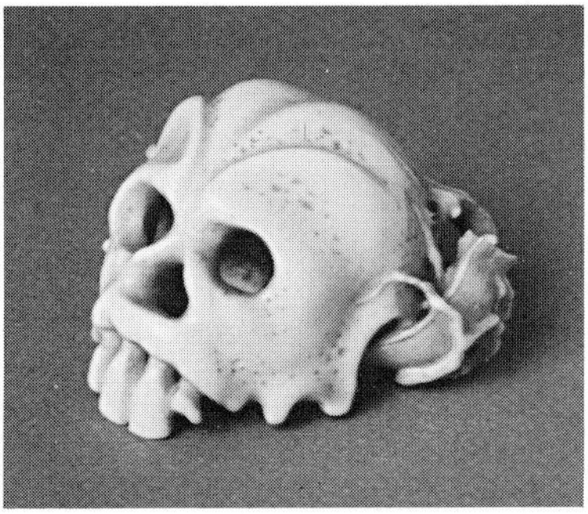

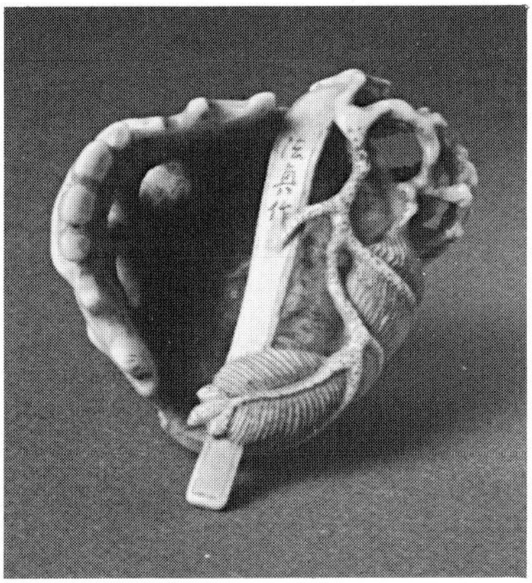

30 Ivory. A freely interpreted skull rests on a branch with leaves and a tablet.
Signed *Hoshin (saku)*.
Hoshin was a mid 19th century artist who specialised in figures.
Museum of the History of Science 2201

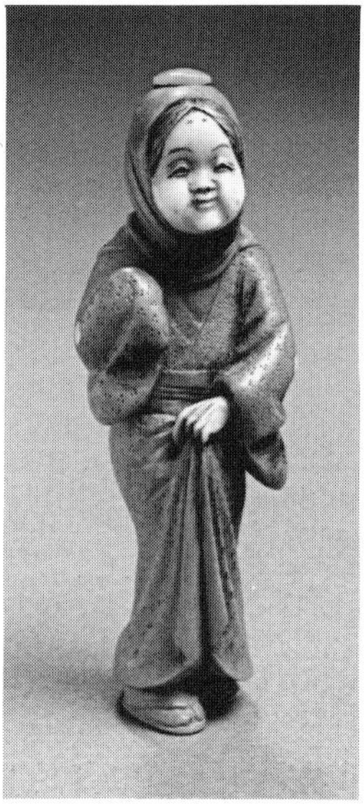

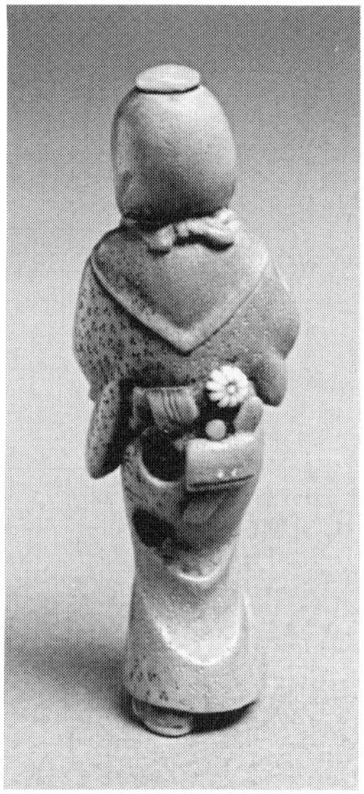

31 Wood, Ivory and coral. A wooden figure of an actor wearing the (ivory) mask of Okame, with her robes clutched around her. There is a coral top-knot on her head, and at her *obi* she wears a tobacco pouch and pipe case suspended from a netsuke. Unsigned. Mid 19th century.

• Okame was the Goddess of Mirth, whose fat smiling face is often found as a noh mask or as a netsuke.

Ashmolean 1956.1736 Ingram gift

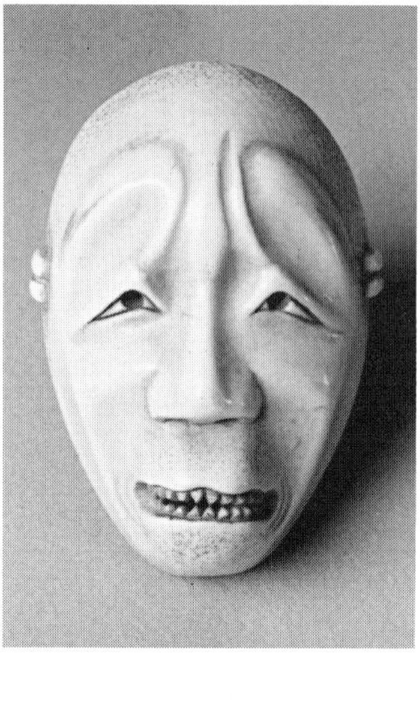

32 Ivory mask. An emaciated and miserable old woman. Some colouring on the lips. Unsigned. 19th century.

• The subject of this idiosyncratic mask has not been securely identified; possibly it represents Uta or Komachi.

Pitt Rivers 2217

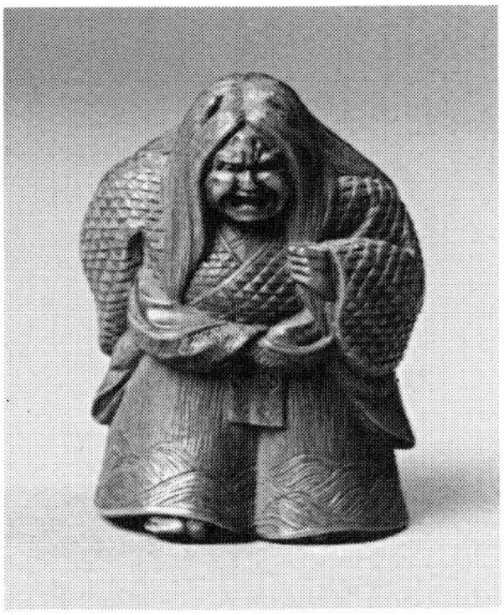

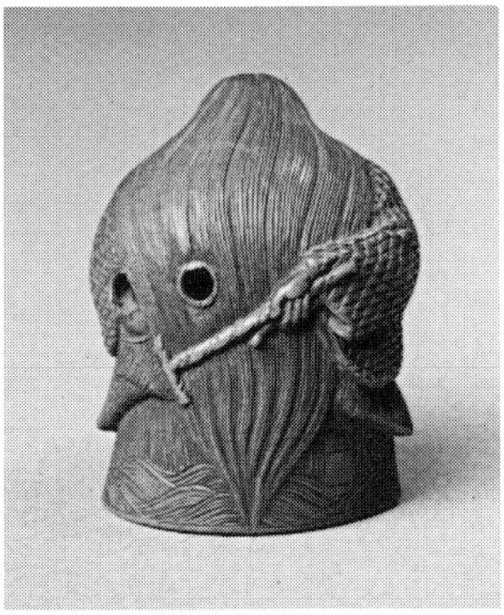

33 Wood. A Noh actor as Kiyohime the witch, with horns in her long hair; she conceals the bell clapper behind her back. The kimono in a raised triangular pattern, and her *tabi* visible beneath. Signed in a rectangular cartouche *Masakazu*. Nagoya school. Mid 19th century.

• Kiyohime as a young woman fell passionately in love with the monk Anchin. He repeatedly rejected her advances, eventually hiding in a temple bell. She thereupon turned into a dragon, caused the bell to fall and trap the unfortunate monk, wound herself around the bell and melted it, incinerating him.
Ashmolean 1956.3263
Ingram gift

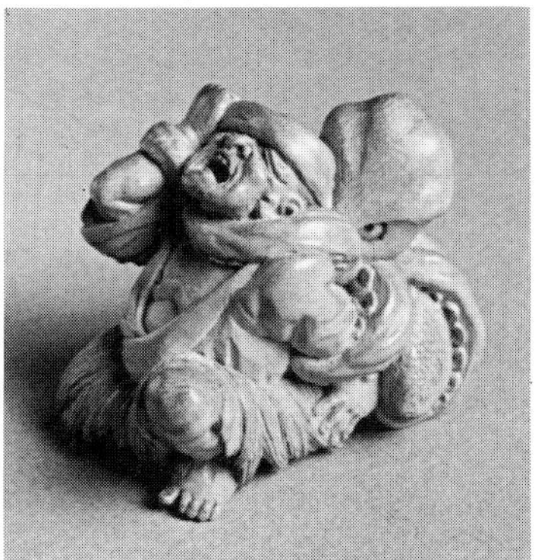

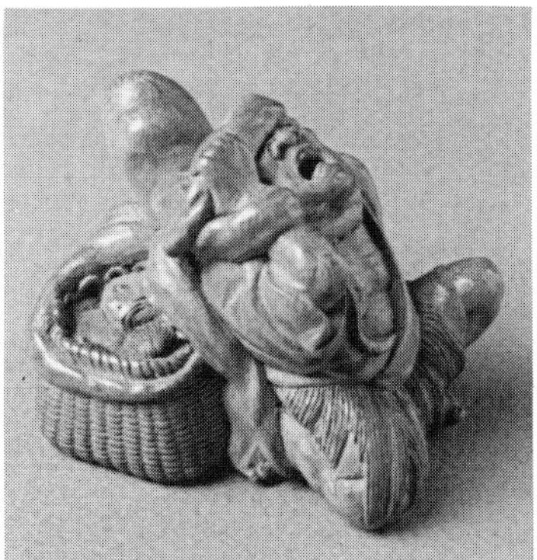

34 Wood. A fisherman struggles desperately to free himself from the embrace of an octopus that has escaped from the basket at his back. The himotoshi under the basket.
Unsigned. 19th century.

• The octopus is quite commonly found as a netsuke, usually struggling amorously with a naked awabi fisher-girl.
Ashmolean 1956.3221
Ingram gift

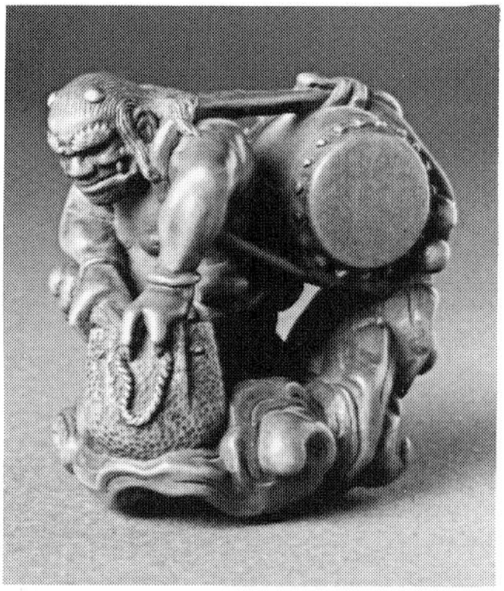

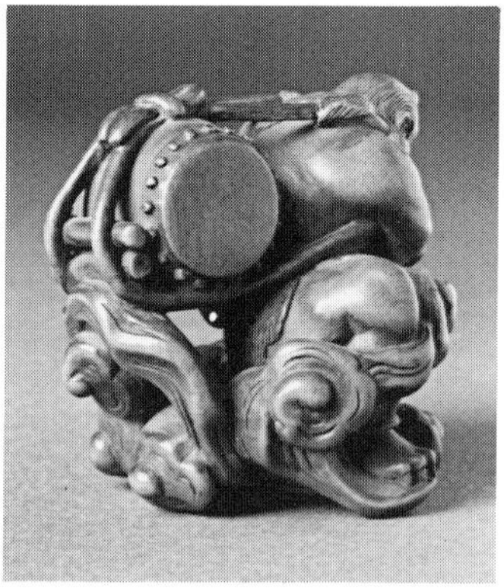

35 Wood. The Thunder Demon, Raiden, his drum on his back crouches as he pulls the winds out of a bag held in his left hand, and the winds swirl about his feet, forming the himotoshi.
Signed *Tomokazu*, incised.
Kano Tomokazu was an early to mid 19th century artist from Gifu.
• Raiden is often found in company with Fujin, the Demon of Wind (see 36). Perhaps their most celebrated depictions are those on screens by Sotatsu and Korin.
Ashmolean 1956.1721
Ingram gift

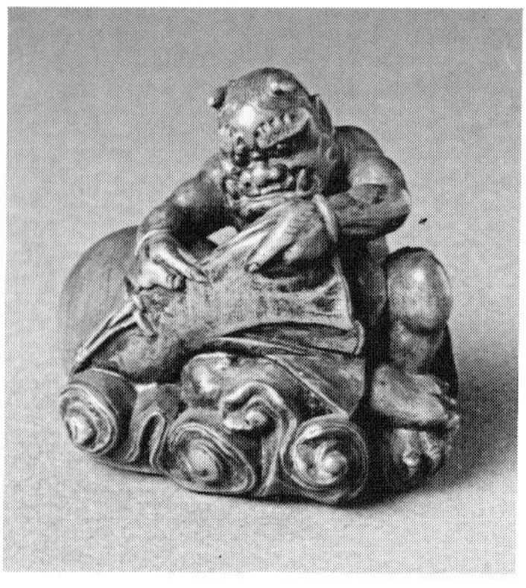

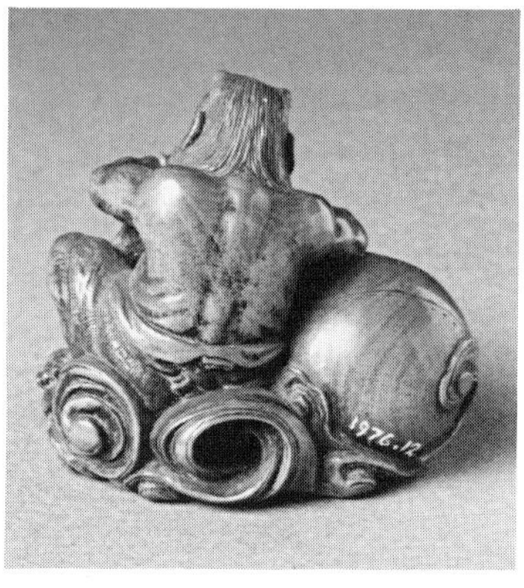

36 Wood. The Wind Demon, Fujin, letting loose the winds from a great bag at his right, the winds swirling about his feet and forming the himotoshi.
Incised signature *Ittan* (d.c.1877).
A Nagoya carver, Ittan specialised in wood figures.
• See 35. Ashmolean 1976.12
Christie-Miller gift

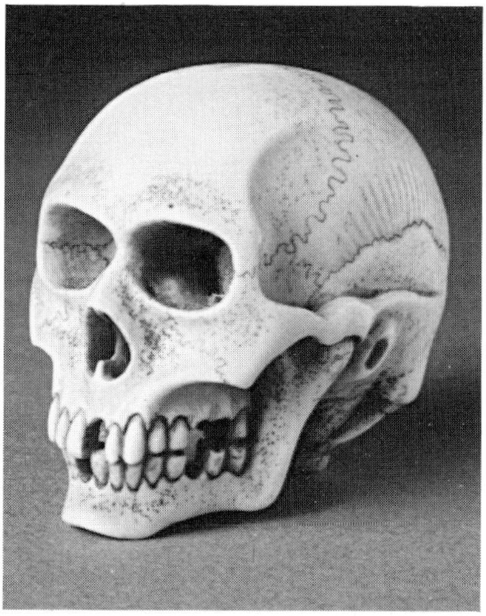

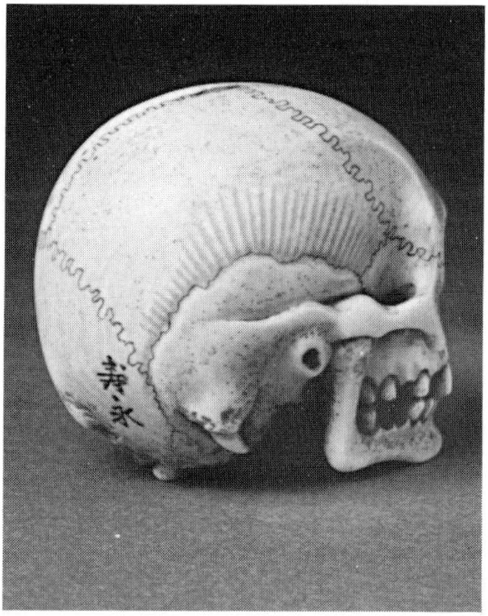

37 Ivory. A large and accurately modelled human skull.
Signed *Toshinaga*.
Kojima Toshinaga worked in Edo during the middle to latter parts of the 19th century.
Museum of the History of Science 644

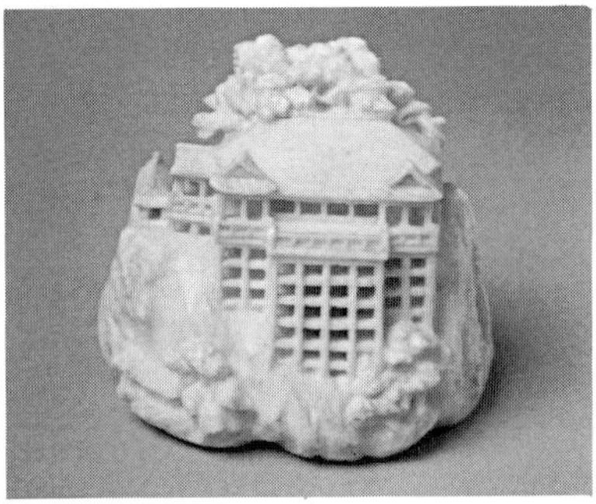

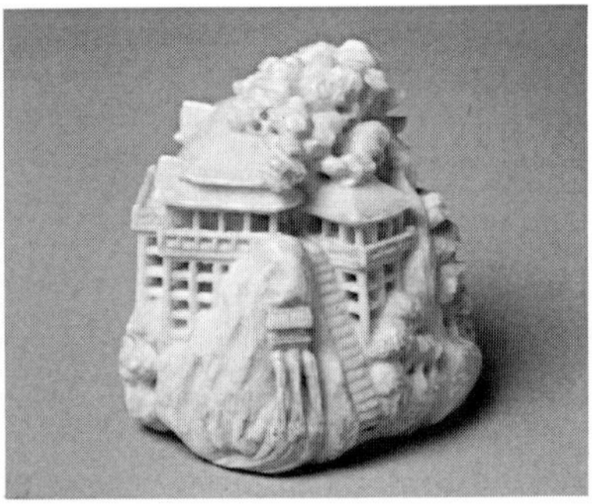

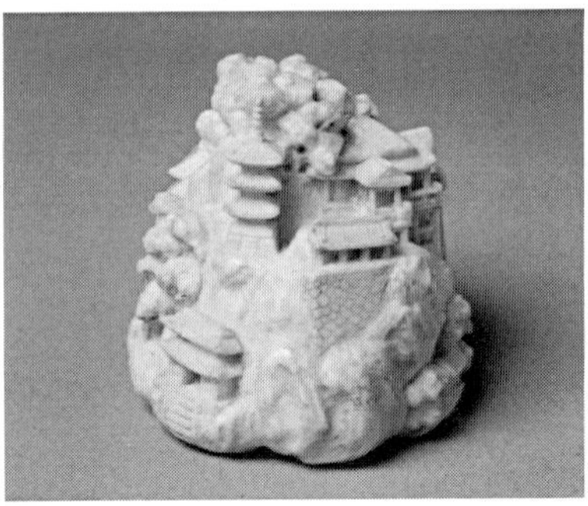

38 Ivory. A landscape carving depicting the Kiyomizu dera in Kyoto, in the round, with deep relief carving.
Signed *Kagetoshi*.
Kagetoshi was a Nagoya carver famous for his minute carvings, often of buildings either real or imaginary.

- It is most unusual to find a readily identifiable place – even one as obvious and as famous as the Kiyomizu-dera – depicted as a netsuke.

Pitt Rivers 1844

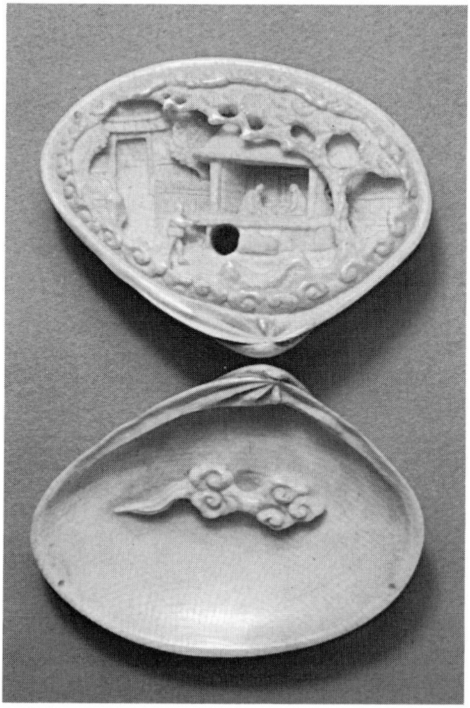

39 Ivory. A clam in two parts; the cord hole leads through the under shell to attach to the upper. The lower shell as two sages seated in a pavilion, with an attendant, with trees and fences and a torii in the background. Unsigned. Late 19th century.
This is an essay in the style of Kagetoshi, the Kyoto and Nagoya carver famous for his minute detail. See 38.
Pitt Rivers 679

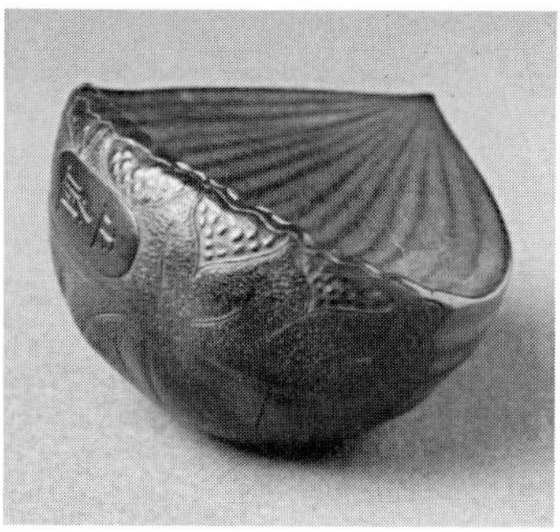

40 Wood. A chestnut realistically carved, with one side concave, and with raised irregular ribbing.
Signed in an oval cartouche *Masanao*.
Masanao worked in Ise, Yamada province, 19th century.
Ashmolean 1956.3277
Ingram gift

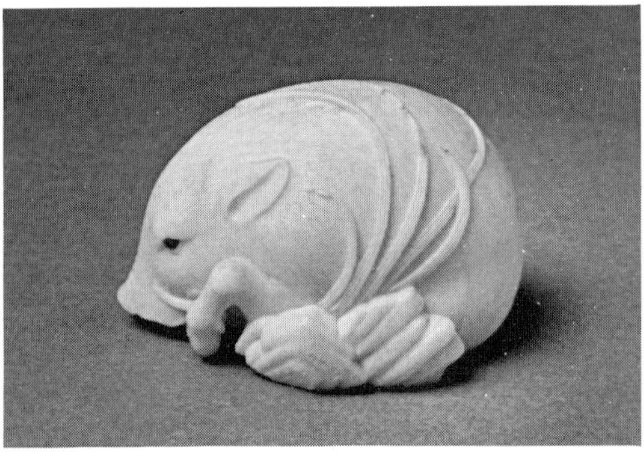

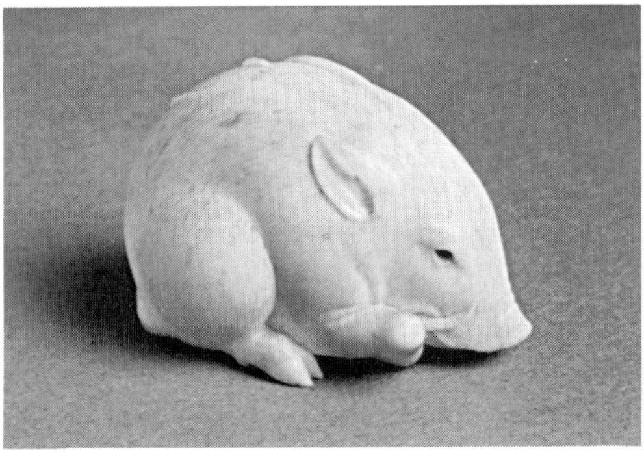

41 Ivory. A wild boar crouches beside rocks, with grasses arching over his back. His feet are tucked up or underneath, one of them forming the himostoshi, and the hair is finely incised. The eyes are inlaid in coral.
Signed in a rectangular cartouche *Kaigyoku,* with seal *Masatsugu.*
Kaigyokusai (1813–1892) was certainly one of the greatest of netsuke carvers. Such was his fame during his lifetime, that his netsuke and okimono were prized by the greatest families in Japan, including the Imperial family. He was always able to select the best quality ivory, which was a necessity for his meticulous and careful style.
• A similar figure in the Victoria & Albert Museum (A940–1910) is illustrated by Earle plate 38. This model is not uncommon and it is highly unlikely that all the known signed examples, even those of high quality, were carved by the master.
Ashmolean 1956.3208
Ingram gift

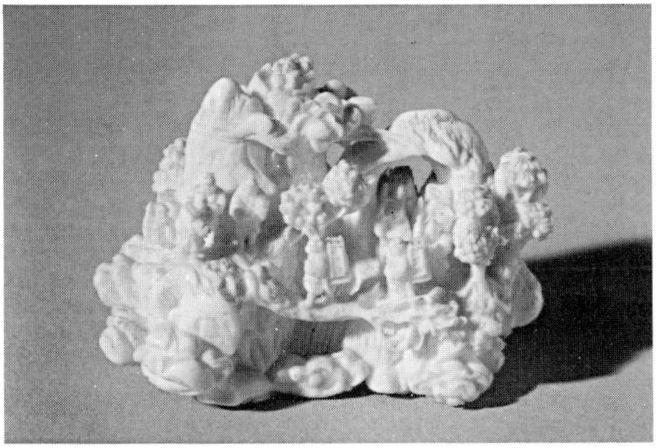

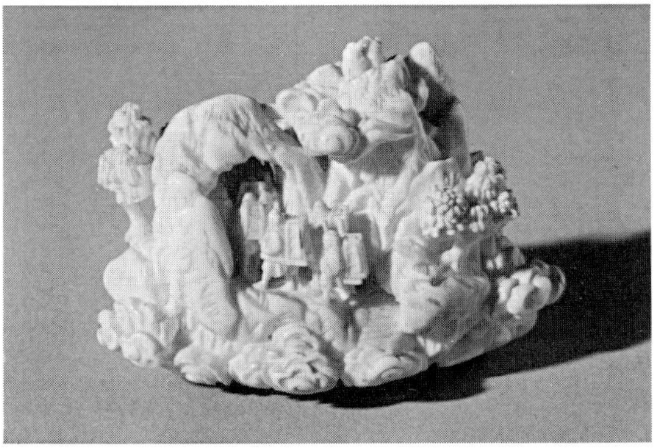

42 Ivory. A minutely carved landscape, depicting a party of 10 Yamabushi passing over a natural archway, to be met by three other persons. Trees and rocks surround them and there are two monkeys at the top. The underside as swirling waves.
Signed on a raised tablet *Kaigyokusai*.
For this celebrated artist, see also 41.

- The Yamabushi were wandering monks who were resident at no particular temple.

Pitt Rivers 2035

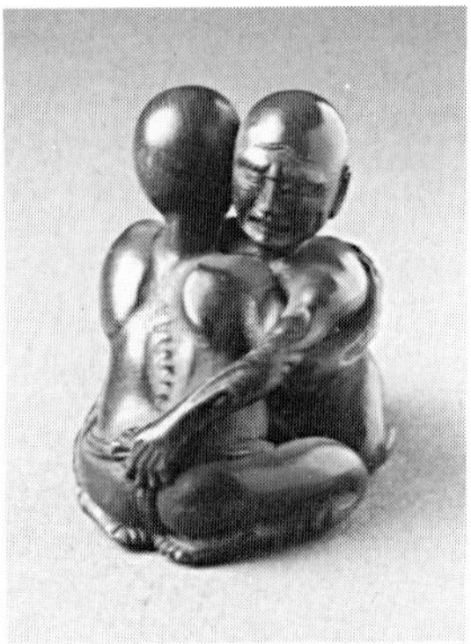

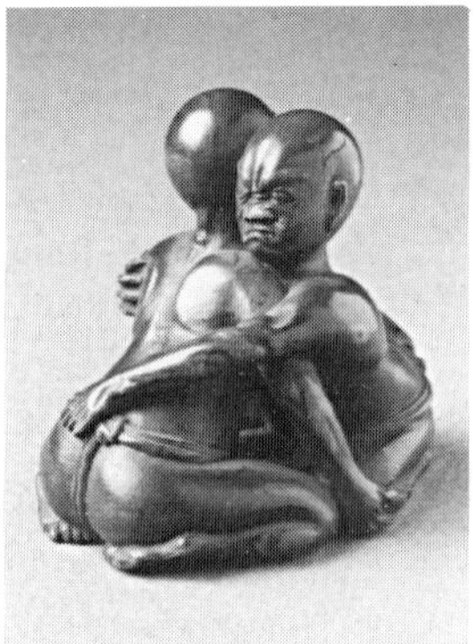

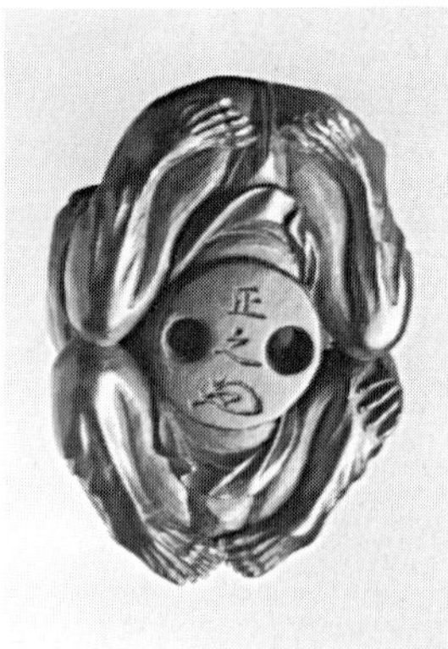

46 Wood. Two thin blind wrestlers kneeling on the ground, reach around each other to grasp the back of the other's loincloth.
Signed *Masayuki* with *kakihan*.
Hoshunsai Masayuki was an Asakusa school artist (see 45–49) who worked mostly in stagshorn; other, fully signed examples of his works in wood, as here, are known – see eg Davey Nos. 546 and 547.
Museum of the History of Science 1929.

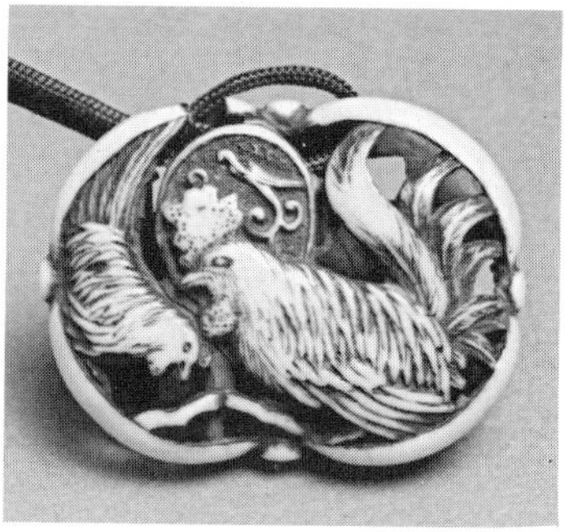

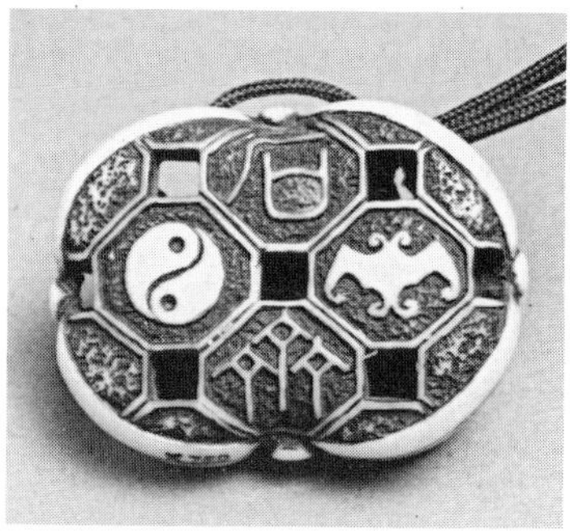

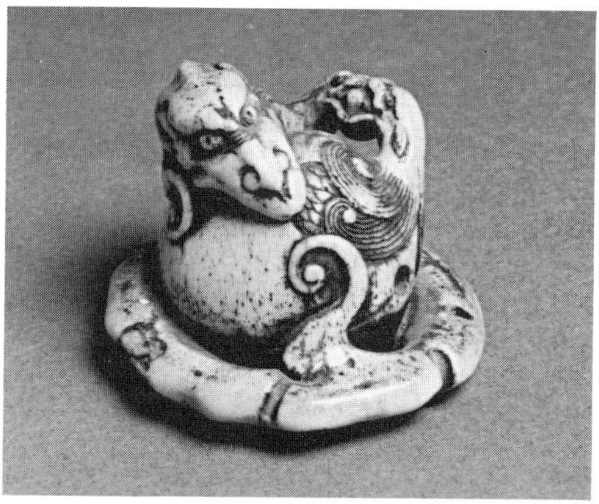

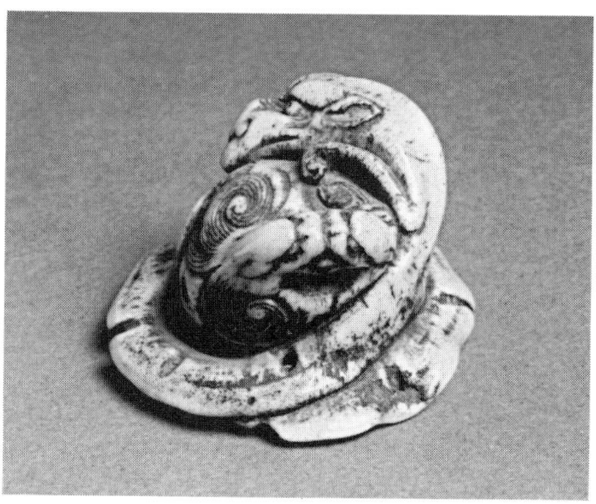

47 Ivory Manju. Pierced with two cockerels before a dragon medallion, the reverse with hexagons and squares carved with a yin-yang symbol and a bat, and with the raised characters Sekisai.
Signed *Sekisai*.
An Asakusa school carving by an unknown maker.
- The signature is particularly abbreviated and difficult to read.

Ashmolean Museum x752
Hildburgh gift

48 Stagshorn. A Dragon coiled round a *mokugyo* bell.
Unsigned.
The eccentric carving of this netsuke, the Buddhist bell and dragon motif identify this as an Asakusa school work, close to that of Kokusai (see 45).
Ashmolean 1956.1732
Ingram gift

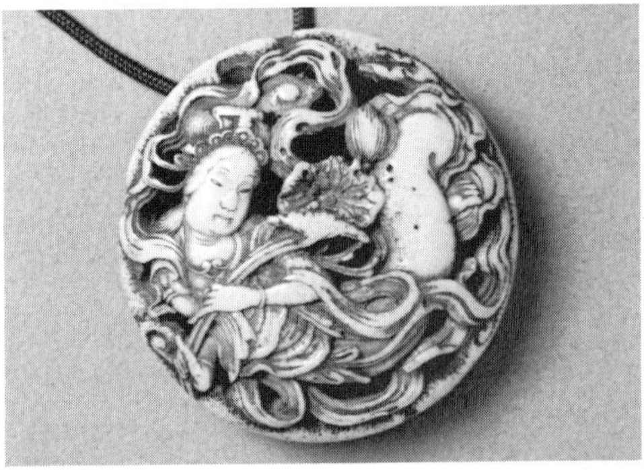

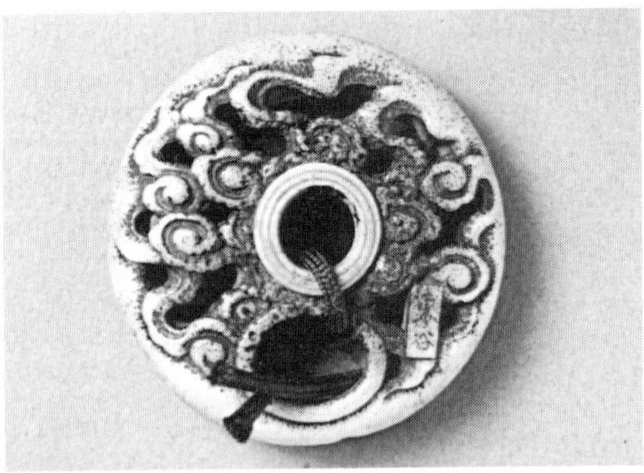

49 Stagshorn manju. A *tennin* bearing a lotus drifts through clouds pierced through the netsuke. The himotoshi at the back.
Signed in a rectangular cartouche *Tokoku*.
Tokoku (1846–1913) was an Asakusa carver known to have been influenced by Kokusai (see 45). Later in life he was famous for his inlaid work, so that this piece, with its stagshorn material and general 'pure' Asakusa feel must surely come from early in his career.
Ashmolean x626

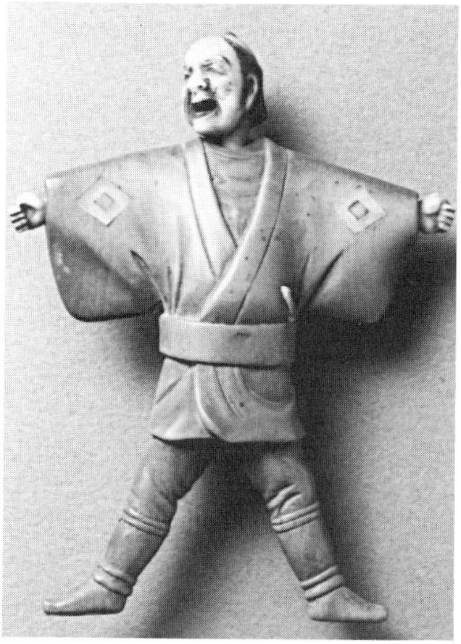

50 Wood and bone. A man standing on splayed legs, toes pointed outwards, with his arms stretched out sideways with his sleeves hanging down, the bone hands and head movable. There is a dagger *(tanto)* thrust through his *obi* and a diamond-shaped *mon* inlaid in horn on the back of his kimono.
Incised signature *Sanshō*.
Kokeisai Sansho (1871–1936) worked in Osaka in wood or ivory, sometimes using the Shibayama technique of inlay.
• There is some suggestion here of a *tatebina* doll, made of folded paper.
Ashmolean 1956.3205
Ingram gift

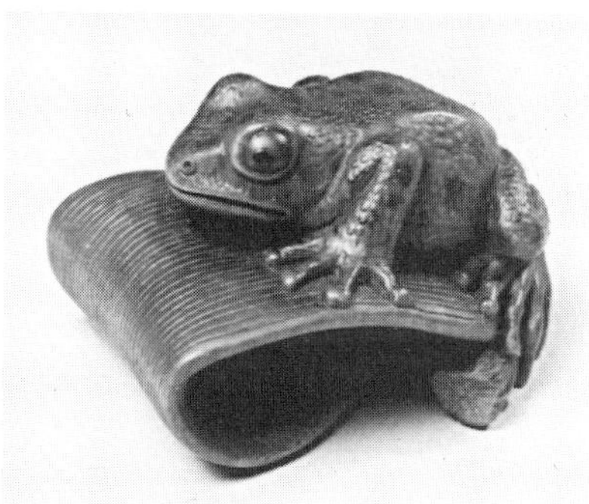

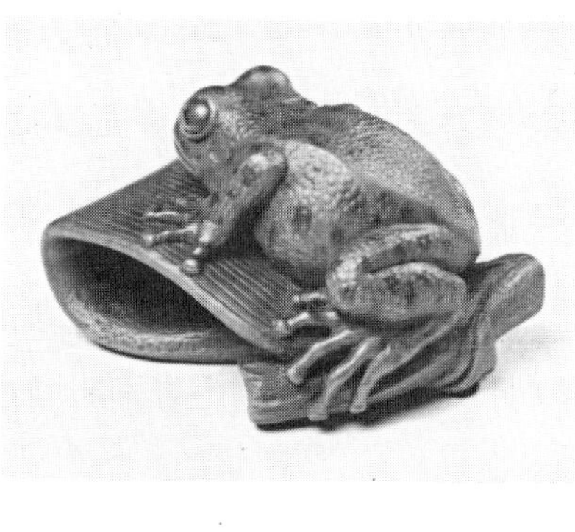

51 Wood. A tree frog crouches on a curled striated leaf. The markings are stained and raised in *ukibori* technique.
Signed in *ukibori* technique *MW* (Michael Webb) *carved at Cropton*.
Michael Webb is one of the leading Western carvers of netsuke. He specialises in boxwood carvings of animals and can be especially noted for his fine detail, and his mastery of the *ukibori* technique. In 1983 he had a one-man exhibition in the Ashmolean Museum; see the catalogue by Oliver Impey.
Ashmolean 1984.6
Gift of the artist

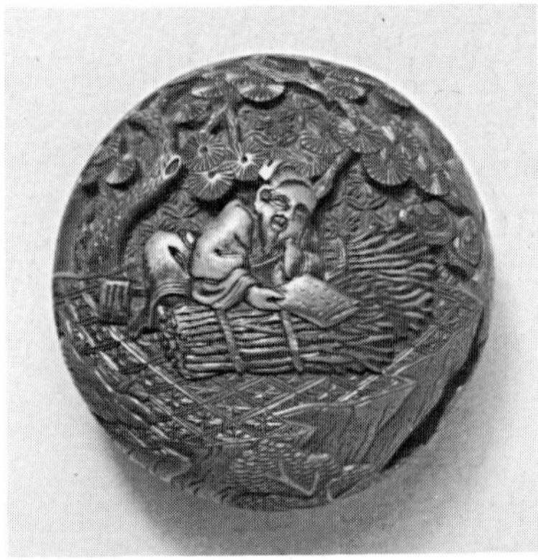

52 Lacquer manju with soft metal additions. A sage sits on two bundles of brushwood, reading, all in shibuichi and gold inlay, on a lacquer manju carved in relief as trees and rocks.
Unsigned. Early 19th century.
Pitt Rivers 1305

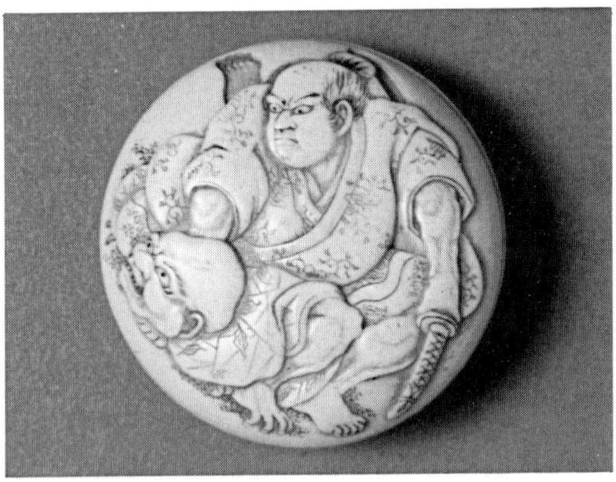

53 Ivory manju. A hero, possibly Raiko, subdues a bald-headed *bakemono*, forcing him to the ground; in relief. The back detachable to reveal the himotoshi attachment.
Incised signature *Koju*, with *kakihan* as a crane.
19th century.
For a comparable example of this Hojitsu (Edo) school artist's work see Davey no. 456.
• Raiko was a celebrated slayer of goblins and ogres; his greatest feat was the killing of the earth-spider.
Ashmolean x629

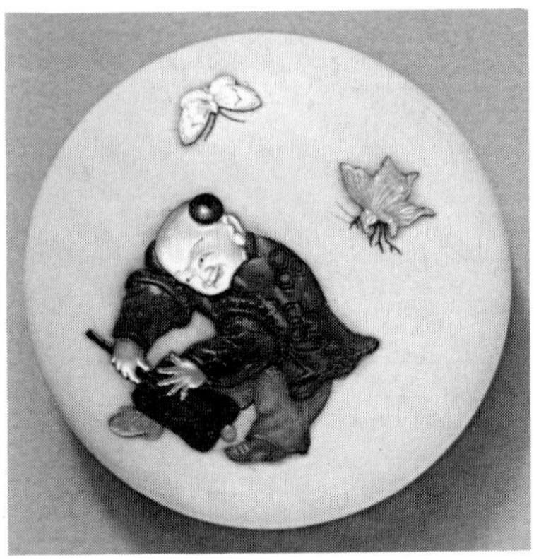

54 Ivory manju with relief inlays in ivory, tortoiseshell, coral and pearl shell in Shibayama style. A Chinese boy with a fan, and butterflies.
Signed on a pearl-shell plaque *Shibayama Yasunobu saku*.
Inlays of this style, into ivory, were a speciality of the Shibayama family. Many of these pieces are of impressive size and complexity. Yasunobu seems to have specialised in manju netsuke.
Pitt Rivers 1302

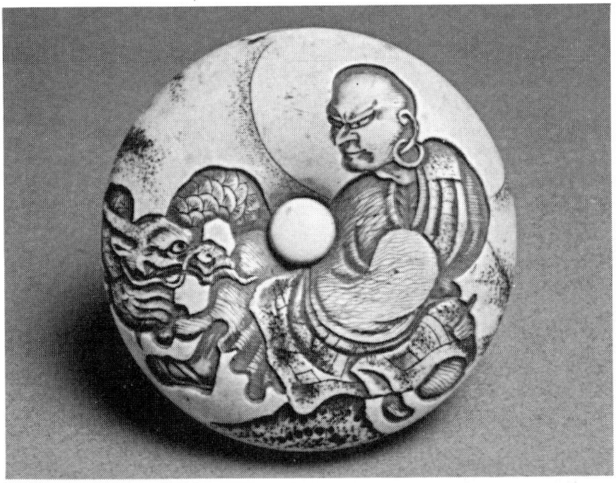

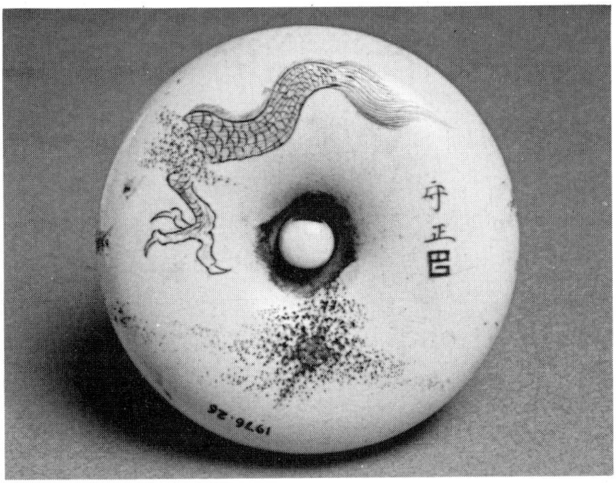

55 Manju, ivory. The *arhat* Handaka Sonja with his familiar dragon, incised. The cord attachment as a plug through the centre of the manju.
Signed *Morimasa* with *kakihan*.
Gyokosai Morimasa worked in Edo in the mid to late 19th century, specialising in manju.
Ashmolean 1976.26
Christie-Miller gift

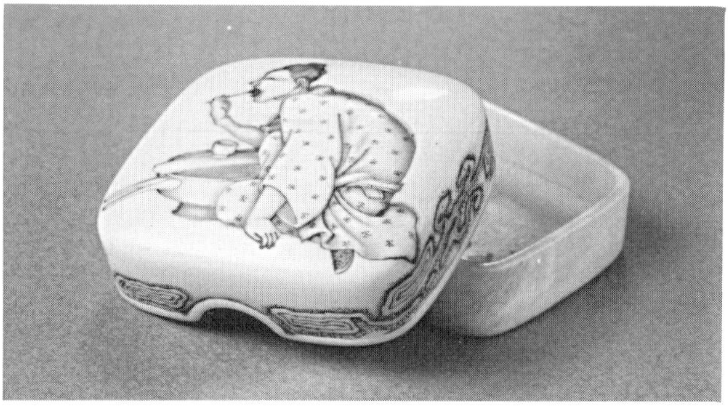

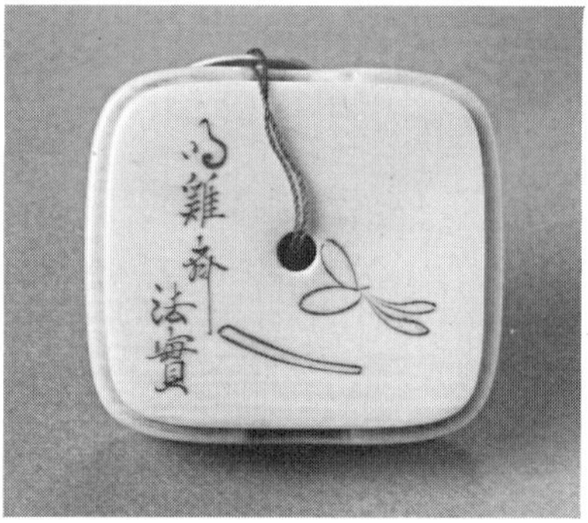

56 Ivory, shaped as a box manju. Low relief carving of a woman, seated before a hot-water pot (*tsuno-darai*), applying blackening to her teeth. Signed *Meikeisai Hojitsu*. Hojitsu (d.1872) was considered in his lifetime to be among the best of the Tokyo carvers.

- It was customary for newly married women to blacken their teeth.

Museum of the History of Science 1936

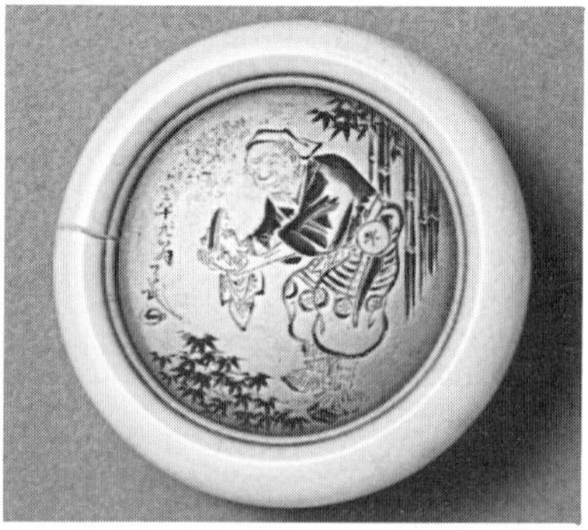

57 Kagamibuta, ivory with soft metal plate. An elderly peasant in a bamboo grove holds in his hands a miniature figure of a woman, incised in a shibuichi ground.
Signed *Temmin at the age of 69*.
Temmin was active in Tokyo circa. 1830–43, specialising in manju netsuke.

- The story is that of the bamboo-cutter who found the Moon-child in a node of bamboo.

Ashmolean 1956.3245
Ingram gift

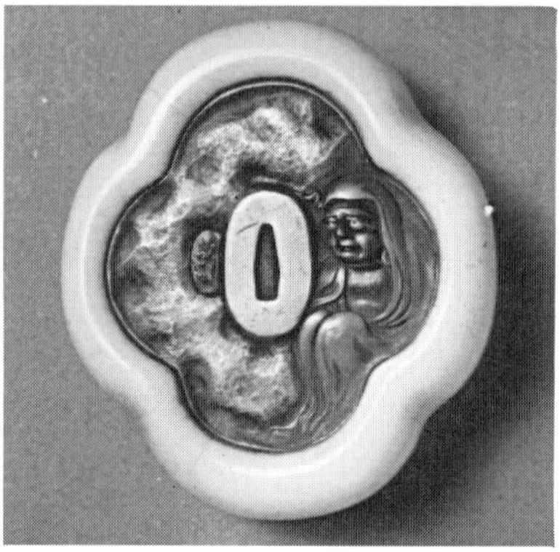

58 Kagamibuta, ivory with soft metal plate in mokko shape, as a tsuba. Daruma in soft metal relief on a sentoku ground.
Unsigned. 19th century. (See 14 and 15).
Ashmolean x1337
Oppenheim gift

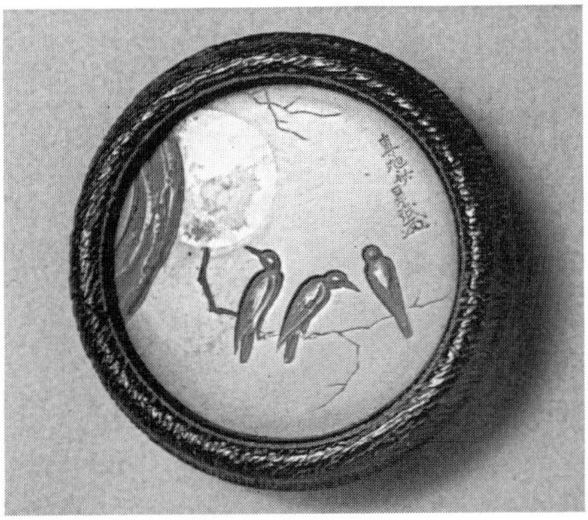

59 Kagamibuta, wood with soft metal plate. Three incised crows on a branch before a silver moon on shakudo ground.
Incised signature *Jukyokusai Riomin* with *kakihan*.
19th century.
Ashmolean x1341
Oppenheim gift

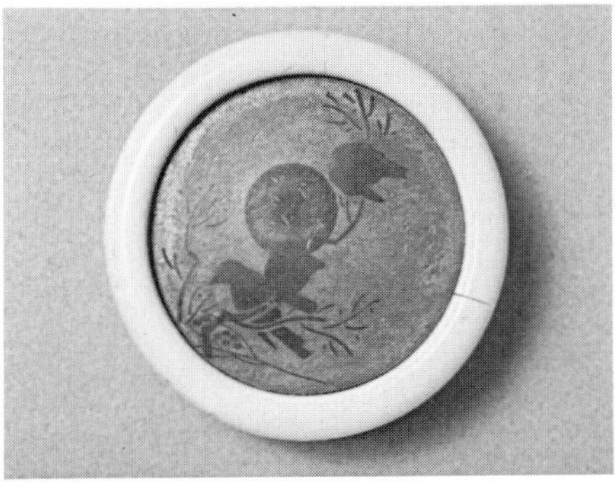

60 Kagamibuta, ivory with soft metal plate. Three shakudo crows perch on a tree before a shibuichi full moon, on silver ground.
Unsigned. 19th century.
Ashmolean 1961.5

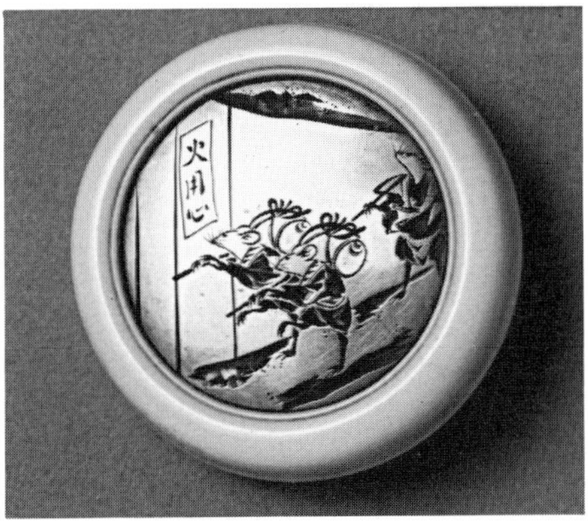

61 Kagamibuta, ivory with soft metal plate. Two rats dressed in kimono, bearing rice bales, followed by a third, pass a doorpost inscribed with the characters *'kayoshin'*, 'Beware of fire', incised on a shibuichi ground.
Unsigned. 19th century.
Ashmolean 1956.3239
Ingram gift

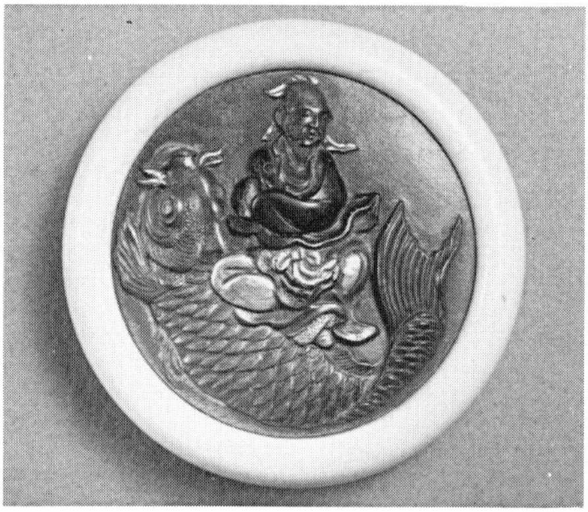

62 Kagamibuta, ivory with soft metal plate. Repoussé relief and inlays, an old man (Kinko) riding on a carp. Unsigned. 19th century.

• Kinko, a Chinese recluse, rode to the river-world on the back of a carp.

Ashmolean 1956.3253
Ingram gift

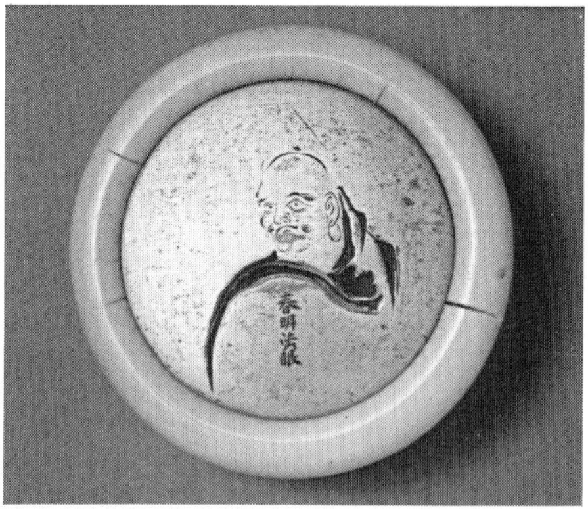

63 Kagamibuta, ivory with gilded plate. Daruma. (See 14 and 15). Inscribed *Haruaki Hogen*. 19th century.

• Not by the sword-fitting maker of this name, but after his style.

Ashmolean x1330
Oppenheim gift

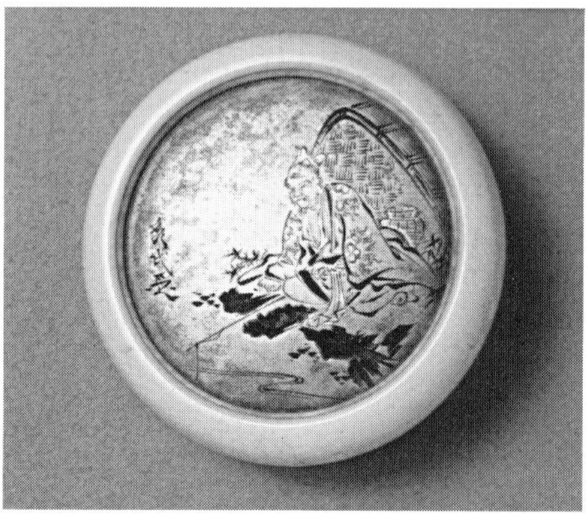

64 Kagamibuta, ivory with soft metal plate. The sage Taikobo sits fishing before a bamboo shelter, in which stands a large sake jar, incised and inlaid on a shibuichi ground. Signed *Shumin*.

• Not Hara Shumin, the artist of 14.

Ashmolean 1956.3247
Ingram gift

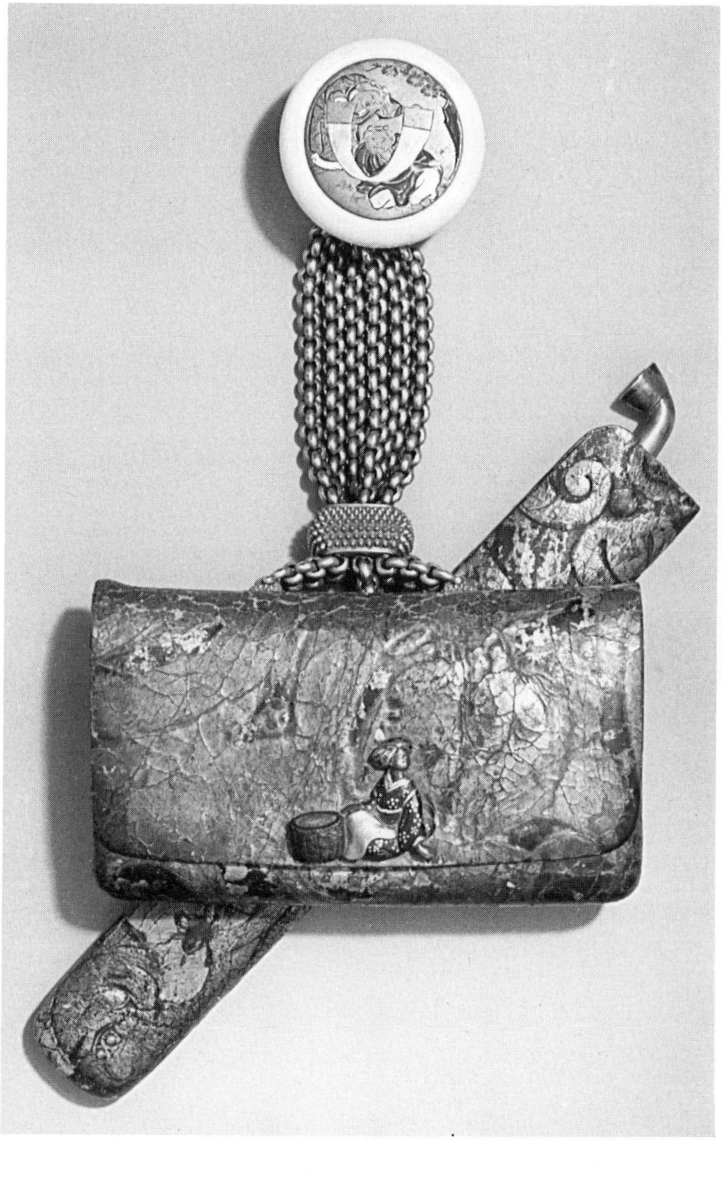

65 A stamped leather tobacco pouch and pipe case, with metal clasp signed Minkoku, suspended by a multiple chain from a Kagamibuta with ivory cup, the plate incised and inlaid with Kanzan and Jittoku reading a scroll on a shibuichi ground.
Signed *Minkoku at the age of 64*.
Riusai Minkoku was an Edo artist specialising in fittings for tobacco pouches.

- The stamped leather is almost certainly a re-used piece of Spanish or Flemish workmanship. This was apparently much admired in the Edo period and later.
- The *sennin* Kanzan and Jittoku are usually shown together, looking at a scroll. They spoke together in a language of their own, and are regarded as the exemplars of eccentricity.

Ashmolean 1986.24
Smethurst gift

Glossary of Japanese terms

arhat	followers of Sakyamuni who have achieved immortality; there are 16 who are most commonly depicted as netsuke.
awabi	*Haliotis* a mollusc prized for the table and for its shell.
bakemono	ghosts, goblins and other supernatural beings.
chonin	the townsmen, middle class.
eboshi	a court hat.
go	a board game.
go	assumed work-name of an artist.
haiyu	an actor.
himotoshi	the holes in a netsuke through which runs the suspension cord.
hirazogan	low-relief inlay into metal.
inro	a medicine box of (usually) tiered compartments hung from the *obi* and kept in place by a netsuke.
jui	a fungus sceptre, mark of rank.
kagamibuta	a flattened netsuke, often as an ivory or wooden cup enclosing a metal plate.
kakihan	the personal mark of an artist, as a written seal.
katabori	a netsuke of basically rounded form – the most common type of netsuke.
katakiri	cutting into metal to imitate brush-strokes.
kimono	the traditional dress of Japan.
kinchaku inro	a money purse suspended as an inro.
manju	a 'bean cake' netsuke, rounded and often carved in low relief.
mokko	a four lobed shape, as a rectangle with indented corners.
mokugyo	a wooden bell-like gong used by Buddhist priests.
mon	family crest.
moxa	a medicine burned as a pellet on the skin.
myoga	ginger.
nio	guardian of a temple gate.
obi	the broad belt worn around the waist.
okimono	a small carving, often little bigger than a netsuke, that is not worn as a netsuke, but stood up.
oni	a demon who can be repelled by the throwing of beans.
ronin	a master-less warrior.
sake	rice-wine.
samurai	the hereditary warrior class.
sashi	an elongated netsuke that hangs over the *obi*.
sennin	ascetics who have achieved magical powers; certain few among a great number are the more commonly depicted as netsuke.
sentoku	brass.
shakudo	an alloy of silver, treated to look almost black.
shibayama	the name of a family of craftsmen who specialised in a technique of inlays of coral, horn etc. into ivory and hence the technique itself.
shibuichi	a pale grey alloy of silver.
shikoro	neck-guards of a helmet.
shishi	lion-dog.
sujibachi	a ridged helmet bowl, where the rivets of the plates do not show.
tabi	socks with divided toes and hardened soles.
takazogan	high-relief inlay into metal.
tanto	a short dagger.
tatebina	folded-paper doll.
tennin	beautiful winged maidens who live in the Buddhist paradise.
torii	the gateway before a Shinto shrine.
tsuba	a sword-guard.
tsuno-darai	a water pot with elongated side handles.
ukibori	a carving technique in wood, whereby an area is depressed by pressure, the surrounding area is carved away, and the depressed area raised by wetting it with water, which swells the wood so it stands proud of its surroundings.
yamabushi	wandering monks or mountain ascetics.

Select bibliography

Barker, Richard and Lawrence Smith 'Netsuke. The miniature sculpture of Japan'. British Museum, London 1976 p. 184.

Bushell, Raymond (ed.) 'The netsuke handbook of Ueda Reikichi', Vermont & Tokyo 1961 p. 325.

Bushell, Raymond 'Collectors' netsuke' New York & Tokyo 1971 p. 199.

Bushell, Raymond 'Netsuke familiar and unfamiliar' New York & Tokyo 1975 p. 259.

Coullery, Marie-Thérèse and Martin S. Newstead. 'Netsuke' catalogue of the Baur Collection, Geneva 1977 p. 428.

Davey, Neil K. 'Netsuke. A comprehensive study based on the M.T. Hindson Collection'. London 1982 (revised ed.) p. 566.

Earle, Joe 'An introduction to Netsuke' Victoria & Albert Museum 1980 p. 47.

Impey, Oliver 'Michael Webb, an English carver of Netsuke' catalogue of an exhibition at the Ashmolean Museum, Oxford 1983 p. 24.

Inaba Michitatsu (Tsuryu) 'Soken Kisho' Osaka 1781.

Joly, Henry L. 'Legend in Japanese art'. London & New York 1908 (reprint London) n.d. p. 453.

Joly, Henry L. and Kumasaku Tomita 'Japanese art and handicraft' London 1916, reprinted London 1976 p. 214.

Kinsey, Miriam 'Living masters of netsuke' Tokyo, New York & San Francisco 1984 p. 232.

Lazarnick, George 'Netsuke and inro artists and how to read their signatures' Honolulu 1982, 2 vols p. 1376.

Meinertzhagen, Frederick 'The art of the Netsuke Carver' London 1956 p. 80.

Moss, Paul (ed.) 'Eccentrics in Netsuke' catalogue of an exhibition at Sydney L. Moss Ltd, London 1982 p. 179.

Okada, Barbra Teri 'Netsuke. Masterpieces from the Metropolitan Museum of Art' New York 1982 p. 119.

'Soken Kisho' see Inaba.

Artists represented

The collections

Ashmolean Museum
2, 7, 8, 11, 12, 14, 15, 16, 18, 19, 20, 21, 25, 26, 28, 31, 33, 34, 35, 36, 40, 41, 43, 45, 47, 48, 49, 50, 51, 53, 55, 57, 59, 60, 61, 62, 63, 64, 65.

Museum of the History of Science
1, 5, 6, 9, 10, 13, 17, 24, 29, 30, 37, 44, 46, 56.

Pitt Rivers Museum
3, 4, 22, 23, 27, 32, 38, 39, 42, 52, 54.